OPINIONS AND ARGUMENT

OPINIONS AND ARGUMENT

FROM SPEECHES AND ADDRESSES

OF THE

# EARL OF BALFOUR

*K. G., O. M., F. R. S., etc.*

1910–1927

*Garden City, New York*

DOUBLEDAY, DORAN & COMPANY, INC.

1928

# PREFATORY NOTE

THE persons responsible for planning this volume are my publishers.

The person responsible for selecting its contents is my niece, Mrs. Edgar Dugdale, to whom my grateful thanks are due.

I am myself responsible for the raw material which she has sifted, but for nothing else.

Whether if I had been in her place I should have chosen as she has done is more than doubtful; and as I do not propose either to read the selection itself, or to review the speeches which might have been in it, but are not, I shall never know. I strongly suspect, however, that in this matter she is a far safer guide than I should be. She is probably a better judge of what (if anything) in the way of old speeches the public are likely to tolerate, and will be less embarrassed by the sort of inconsistencies which anxious critics sometimes discover in the public utterances of the least adventurous politicians.

On one point only I would ask the reader's indulgence. My memory on all matters, but especially my verbal memory, is hopelessly defective. For good, therefore, or for evil, the wording of my speeches is of necessity unprepared. Few indeed are those who, in such conditions, can speak as they would write; and certainly I am not one of them.  If it be asked whether the defect in extempore speech could not be cured by subsequent corrections, I reply that it certainly could; but that it would be far more trouble to make the corrections than to make the speech.  Only a small number, therefore, of the following utterances have been amended, or even seen, by me subsequent to their delivery—not more (Mrs. Dugdale informs me) than two. In these cases the fact of correction is noted.

BALFOUR.

*Whittingehame.*
September, 1927.

# CONTENTS

## SECTION I—PERSONAL AND OTHER MEMORIES

## SECTION II—A POLITICAL MISCELLANY

vii

# CONTENTS

## SECTION III—THE MODERN STATE

## SECTION IV—ON IMPERIAL AFFAIRS

## SECTION V—ZIONISM

# CONTENTS

## SECTION VI—INTERNATIONAL AFFAIRS

## SECTION VII—GOLF

SECTION I

PERSONAL AND OTHER MEMORIES

# OPINIONS AND ARGUMENT

I

## ON RESIGNATION OF THE LEADERSHIP OF THE UNIONIST PARTY

*Speech to the Executive Committee of the City of London Conservative Association, November 8th,* 1911

MR. CHAIRMAN,—You have stated, I think quite rightly, that there could not be a more fitting audience to whom I could make the announcement that I propose to make immediately than those who represent my constituency, who gave me a seat in the House of Commons at the moment when the fortunes of our party were at the very lowest, and who thus enable me to do what work I have done for the party since 1906. Therefore it is to them first, and through them to my many friends in all parts of the country, that I desire to say that after very long and serious thought I have come to the conclusion, for reasons which I shall state presently, that the moment has arrived when I ought to resign—not my seat, which I hope you will allow me, as long as you think I can serve you, to retain, but my leadership of the party with which I have been so long connected, and for whose fortunes I still hope to do good service. I do not think that anybody who really knows the facts will grudge me some period of repose, or will think that I am making an unreasonable request in asking, not that I should be released from the public service, but that I should be released from the continuous and unceasing strain which inevitably falls upon a leader of a party at any period of our history, but which falls upon him with increasing severity as the claims of democracy, under our popular form of government, grow and multiply.

I have been nearly thirty-eight years in Parliament. If you count leadership of the Opposition as being equivalent to office itself—for indeed it is equivalent, so far as labours are concerned, to a heavy office—I have been in office, in that broad sense of the word, for a quarter of a century, and for a quarter of a century continuously.

I first joined Lord Salisbury's Cabinet, in 1886, in a position which at that time was one of some administrative difficulty, as Secretary for Scotland. Almost immediately afterwards, in a very few months, I became Irish Secretary—not an easy post. And then, when through the lamented death of my friend, Mr. W. H. Smith, I became Leader of the House of Commons, I began a course of leadership of the party in the House which has lasted for twenty years. These twenty years of leadership of the party in the House included ten years of leadership of the whole House. I was Leader of the House for ten consecutive years—a longer period, I believe, of continuous leadership of the House than that of any Minister since the death of William Pitt.

And of the twenty-five years since I first joined the Cabinet, seventeen were passed, not merely in office in the broad sense in which I used the term, but actually and technically in office in the service of the Crown.

Let me add this, as a sort of indication of the way time has gone on and men have been removed from the scene of these political activities. I do not believe that at this moment there are more than four or five members of the Unionist Party in the House of Commons who have ever worked with any other leader. These are Mr. Chaplin, Mr. Walter Long, Mr. Wortley, Mr. Wyndham—I think, for one or two months—and there may be another, but I am not sure. But I do not believe there are more than five who have ever known what it is to have another leader in the House of Commons.

The work of a leader has always been strenuous, but, as I said just now, it is an increasing work. It is an increasing work for two or three quite different reasons. It is an increasing work because under the peculiar arrangements which commend themselves to his Majesty's present advisers the House of Commons is expected to sit for ten or eleven months in every year, and that throws a tremendous additional strain not only on the Ministers themselves, on the Officers of the House, and the Public Departments, but also necessarily and inevitably upon him, whoever he may be, who

is for the time being responsible for the policy of
the Opposition.   That is one of the causes of the
growing labours of a leader of a party.

The other is that the demands for extra-
Parliamentary work grow each year continuously.
I have been peculiarly fortunate in the last five
years in having represented a constituency which
has never been wanting in kindness and sympathy
to me, and who never threw a single atom of additional or unnecessary labour upon my shoulders.
You, gentlemen, the representatives of the Executive Committee in particular, have relieved me of
the whole strain to which less fortunate Members
of Parliament have to submit.   You have allowed
me to go through the two last General Elections
not, indeed, without severe labours, but, at all
events, without severe labours in your midst,
and for this constituency. Speaking not merely
for myself, but for the party, I am glad to repeat
the expressions of gratitude which I hope have not
been wanting on my part in the past.

But in spite of these peculiarly fortunate circumstances in which I am placed the broad fact
remains, and it is, believe me, one of the dangers
in the future of democracy, that the demand made
upon legislators and administrators for work which
is neither administration nor legislation is becoming so heavy that both legislation and administration are likely to suffer.   And you will more and
more find it difficult to get at the same time men of
adequate leisure, adequate position, prepared to
undergo the great toils which inevitably attach now

to political life. We are probably nearer than we have ever been before to entrusting our affairs to those who for quite worthy, but on the whole, less satisfactory reasons, are prepared to be politicians and nothing but politicians, to work the political machine as professional politicians—not professional in a bad sense or a degrading sense—but still you will find it more and more difficult to obtain from those who are best able to give it, the best kind of public service in the House of Commons and elsewhere.

I do not wish, however, to trespass on these general considerations. I have no right to go beyond my own personal case, but I am sure that however much you may share the regret which, of course, I feel in bringing to a conclusion so long and so closely packed a page of my life as that occupied in my leadership, even you will not grudge me the desire I have for some diminution in the political burden which has so long rested upon my shoulders.

You may say that I am not yet sixty-four and that I ought to have, if my health is spared, many years of active life before me. About that no man can say. Let me make this single observation. I desire to leave the position of heavy responsibility which I have held, before I can be suspected of suffering from the most insidious of all diseases, the disease which comes upon those who, without losing their health or their intellect, nevertheless get somewhat petrified in the old courses which they have pursued, whose authority grows because they have been long in the public service, or have been great men of science or business, or whatever it may be, but who cannot deal with the great problems which, in this changing world, are perpetually arising, with all the freshness and elasticity really desirable in those who have to conduct great concerns.

No man ever knows in himself when that moment has come. A man knows when he is ill; a man may even know when his memory begins to fail, or see some other obvious sign of decay rest upon his vision. But the sort of malady of which I am speaking may attack people in the prime of life, in the prime of intellectual vigour, as long as the intellectual vigour is exercised along the old lines, but nevertheless, although they may retain apparently all the powers both of brain and of limb which they had in the prime of life, they are less capable of adapting themselves to changing cir-cumstances than those who are of less authority because younger, and yet are more capable also because younger. I am vain enough to hope, though no man can tell, that I have not reached that period, but I should be miserable if I ran the margin fine; and nothing, I think, would be more terrible than to realise that while people were looking to you more than ever, owing to your lengthening experiences —looking to you for leadership—you had not got the keenness of vision or the alertness, which must go with increasing years, adequately to meet the demands which are made upon you.

Now, if I have carried you with me so far in

this somewhat egotistical exposition of the situation, you will observe that really the only problem is this: If the fortunes of our party were to rise—as I think they will—to their ancient height, I have not, I am confident, the vigour again to conduct a Ministry. If that be so, and if we are in sight of a time when my term of leadership must come to an end, the only question for me to consider is when is the best time to go, from a party point of view; and I have no doubt, after having given the matter the most careful consideration that I can, that this is the best time. All times are bad. If a surgical operation is to be performed, to-morrow always seems a better day than to-day.

But the reason I say that to-day is the right time is that if I were to put if off, for example, till next Session, I should be told, and told with some justice, "You have chosen a moment when the party is face to face with a great controversy on Home Rule, on Disestablishment, on Universal Suffrage"—and heaven knows what, because the programme of the Government increases daily as their capacity for carrying it through by legitimate means diminishes. I should be told that there could not be a worse opportunity for resigning, with such a contest immediately before us, and I think that would be true. A change of leadership must always produce some disturbance, however slight, and it would be wrong of me to make such a change—it might be made inevitable by an attack of illness at any moment—it would be wrong of me to make that change at any crisis when the great causes that we have at heart were really being fought over in the House of Commons.

This Session is, relatively speaking, an uncontroversial Session. There is plenty of debate and plenty of legitimate criticism of the Government policy, but still those who know about politics will readily understand how broad is the distinction between a Session like the autumn Session we are now engaged upon, with only the Insurance Bill among the big Government novelties to deal with, and next Session, when we are threatened by all these revolutionary suggestions. Therefore, I say, this Session, not next; and if you say to me, "But why cannot you wait over till next Session, till the Home Rule controversy is over?"—I reply, who knows what is going to happen before the end of next Session? Who knows whether we shall not be in the throes of a General Election? And what chance has my unfortunate successor if he has no time to get into his saddle, if he is given no interval before the stress of fight comes on us, and if he is suddenly left in the very crisis of our destinies to deal with a situation which he had never been able to survey or to contemplate?

The only other argument against choosing this moment is that in the opinion of some people, at least, there is a certain feeling of unrest in the party. Believe me, my experience is a long one, and it has been lengthened by a careful reading of the constitutional history of this country before I entered Parliament. I do not believe at this moment that there is anything exceptional in the state of the party. If you choose to look at the position of the Conservative Party, let us say, two years before Mr. Disraeli's great triumph in 1874; if you choose to look at the position of the Radical Party two years or three years before Mr. Gladstone's great triumph of 1880; if you choose to look at the position of the Conservative Party (it was not Unionist then), when we had all those regrettable difficulties connected with the National Union, which some here may remember, in 1883—and that was before the great triumph of 1886; if you look at the condition of the Radical Party, with the Liberal Imperialists, with all the divisions and the opposition of policy by which they were afflicted in the early years of this century, before their unexampled triumph of 1906, I think you will agree with me that, as compared with other parties which have been long out of office, and suffered defeats at the poll, we are not in the bad condition which some over-critical advisers would suppose.

Remember, parties are made up of human beings, and from the very nature of the case there will always be people, when things are not going right, who grumble and who criticise. It is inevitable, and nobody ought to lose their tempers over it. Such critics are like the microbe which (so doctors tell us) always dwells within our organism. If we sit in a draught, or lower our vitality by fatigue, we get a violent cold in the head and a slight fever, but when our strength is recovered the microbe resumes its proper place, becomes comparatively innocuous, and the full vigour of the patient is restored. So let nobody take a dark view of our fortunes.

On the contrary—and it is one of my reasons for choosing this moment—I believe that we have before us a prospect of growing influence in the country. We are on the upward grade, and I will tell you why I think so. This Government has lived on electoral bribes for six years. They have been floating helplessly down the revolutionary stream, which they have not controlled or guided in any way, snatching now at one electoral advantage and now at another electoral advantage. They have attacked the Crown, they have attacked the Second Chamber, they have bound the Representative Chamber hand and foot; and having finished their bribes, they are now lapsing into the old Radical practice of destroying Churches, passing from the gerrymandering point of view, and generally comporting themselves as a Radical party in difficulties always does comport itself. I do not believe the country will stand it much longer. I believe that I see signs, unless my powers of vision have gone entirely astray, of a steadily growing disgust among all the better classes of the population. And I firmly believe that my successor will have the inestimable advantages in the early days of his office of finding that there is a growing mass of public behind us, and that the great causes that we represent are growing in favour with the mass of our fellow-countrymen.

I do not know that I have anything more to add.

I thank you for your patience. A severance like that which I announce to-day must cause pain to all of us. But it would be, I think, much greater pain, at all events so far as I am concerned, if I felt that I was abandoning political life, if I felt that I was leaving for ever the companionship, the fellowship, and the councils of those with whom, through all these decades, I have worked in perfect harmony and friendship. But it is not so. I hope still to have years of activity which I can devote not merely to the constituency which I represent, but to the whole country, to the whole party, to all who represent the Unionist cause in England, in Scotland, or in Ireland. Those services will not indeed be given under the same arduous conditions as they have hitherto been given. They will not impose the same strain upon my growing years, but I hope they will not be without some small value.

At all events, this I can say, that while men grow old, and men pass, those who have given service must feel, when the time of their service comes to an end, that behind all these individual considerations there are great permanent causes which do not decay with human weakness or perish with human life. And to those great causes I shall be as devoted as your member—I shall do all the service I can as your member—as I have done as the leader of the party, and we may feel ourselves in the future as we have in the past, brethren engaged in the furtherance of one great cause.

## 2

### On War Work

*Speech to the Tenantry of the Whittingehame
Estate on receiving an Address "Commemorat-
ing Lord Balfour's services at the Washington
Conference, and his elevation to the Peerage,"
November 17th, 1922*

I NEED not, I am sure, tell you with what deep
emotions I have received the Address which has just
been read, and how highly I value the feelings which
it expresses. I do not know that either by temperament or training I have any particular appetite for
honours. But, nevertheless, when they have been
given to me by the favour of our Sovereign, and
with the sympathy of my friends in all parts of the
world, it is impossible but that I should receive them
in the spirit in which they were given, and with the
utmost gratitude, and with a deep impression of how
far they exceed any merits to which I can lay claim.

Mr. Wallace referred to an earlier occasion on
which my friend on this estate presented an
Address to me when I became Prime Minister,
rather more than twenty years ago. Those twenty
years have been filled with events of an importance
which no twenty years, I imagine, in the history of
the world has ever exceeded. I am now twenty
years older than I was then, and I cannot feel for a

moment that I have the youthful vigour, or, at all events, the middle-age vigour which I possessed when the first of these Addresses was presented.

To leave the House of Commons is a great severance, I assure you. I sat in it from the beginning of the year 1874 until June, I think it was, in the present year—which really means that all the working days of my life, all the years devoted to public affairs, nearly amounting to half a century, were spent there.

I have held office there. I have been in opposition there. I have been Prime Minister there. I have been Leader of the Opposition there. Those are memories which make it difficult for me to feel the complete and final abandonment of the scene of activities without some of those regrets which all of us entertain, as the lapse of time robs us one by one of the opportunities and the capacities which we enjoy earlier in our lives.

In my case, however, this severance, inevitably painful, was really largely mitigated by the fact that long before I ceased to be eligible to be a member of the House of Commons my work in that assembly had diminished almost to vanishing point. I gave up the leadership of the party to which I had the honour to belong in 1911, and I had then assumed that for the remainder of my life, I might take part in the House of Commons work—and that I was not severed altogether from public affairs. But I never contemplated the possibility of my returning in any capacity to the front line of working politicians.

Nor should I have done so had it not been for
the outbreak of the Great War. That changed the
destinies of half the world, and among that half I
had to count myself. I again felt I had no choice
but to return to active—indeed, most laborious—
public life, first as head of the Admiralty, and then
as head of the Foreign Office. But neither of these
two posts—all important as they were, laborious as
they were—involved any work in Parliament, except
occasionally, and in rare cases.

Then there was the Armistice. For nine months
after that I was over in Paris dealing with the
peace of Versailles, and since then no inconsiderable
fraction of every year has had to be spent out of
this country in connection with the League of
Nations work. Last, but not least, the Washington Conference, which lasted more than three
months.

I enumerate all these changes in my life, not
because they are specially interesting, except from
this point of view—they have conspired, in the first
place, to sever all my connection, or diminish it, with
the House of Commons before it was finally
severed by my taking the peerage; because they conspired to prevent me spending my time here at
home, as I expected to do in 1911. At that time it
was difficult to see any reason which would militate
against that plan. But it has turned out otherwise.
During the war it was hardly possible to be here.
I was confined by my work to the centre of London.
Had it not been that Whittingehame was near the
Firth of Forth, which, being a naval centre, I had

to visit on official business more than once, I should have hardly been able to live in my own home while the war lasted.    And after the war was over, the events to which your attention has been called have kept me not only from Whittingehame, but my own country, to such an extent that I felt that I was an exile from our shores, and was carrying out foreign diplomatic missions rather than those of a Cabinet Minister in his own country.

I hope that unfortunate state of things has now finally come to an end, and that henceforth I may look forward to spending a large part of my time among my friends who have met me here to-day to do me honour. I know my long absence has in no way killed your affection for me and my family. Your affection has remained undiminished by absence, however prolonged, and I am glad to think that those absences will now be fewer in number and of shorter extent, and I may feel, not merely by sentiment but by residence, that I am one unit among those who are assembled here to-day in this room—all those connected with the estate. However that may be—and I don't like to prophesy too confidently about the future—the events of this afternoon have, I hope, brought us even closer together than before. Believe me, what you have done will always remain in my mind as an earnest expression of the warmest feelings; and of a clear proof of that interchange of good feeling which has never ceased to flow between us.

I beg you to accept from me my heartiest and sincerest thanks, and to assure you that I feel from my very inmost being how much I owe to your kindness and good feeling, and what a strength it is to me to complete the unbroken connection which events have not weakened nor distance severed. Ladies and gentlemen, I thank you.

## 3
## On Eton

*Speech at the unveiling of Lord Balfour's own portrait in the School Library by Lord Curzon, Fourth of June, 1921*

THE position of anybody whose portrait is presented in his presence to any great public institution is necessarily one of some embarrassment. I do not know that a position inherently difficult has been made easier by the kindness of the terms in which the presentation has been effected by Lord Curzon. He indeed has spoken with the eloquence to which all his friends are accustomed on a theme which is personal to me and on which I cannot easily dwell or easily make any observations that will not seem out of taste and out of place.

But it is something to be praised by a great Etonian in the presence of a great Etonian audience, for he himself represents so much that is Etonian, that for an old Etonian to be praised by him is to be praised, as I feel, by an expert.

It was another great Viceroy of India and another great Foreign Secretary whose passion for this school was such that he desired to be buried within its precincts, and now he lies in the shadow of its chapel. Lord Curzon has distinguished himself in the same great fields of public administration; he feels, like Lord Wellesley, the same reverent affection for the school of which he was the glory, and to be praised by him before such an audience is a landmark in any man's life.

But behind all that he was good enough to say about me there lay quite plainly that groundwork of belief which is, after all, the reason we are all assembled in this room. He was not so much thinking of the individual; he was thinking of the great institution, the great school of which he and I were members, and with which all of you in one way or other are connected, and it is the spirit of that school which really is the thing worth considering, and worth reflecting on, on such an occasion as this. He described with perfect accuracy my undramatic career within the precincts of the school; he described in eloquent terms, eloquent but not excessive, the debt which, as he thinks, he and I owe alike to the years we spent here.

Certainly there is something about Eton which no other school, or any other institution, I believe, in the world possesses in equal measure. It is hard to define; it is probably indefinable.

Our Eton poet has given expression to the material charm which Eton eternally possesses, and has clearly indicated what in his view is no more than the truth, that the ancient buildings and the famous river carry with them from generation to generation of schoolboys some peculiar virtue, some unforgettable grace, but he has not dwelt on it; it did not lie within the compass of the famous ode. He had not dwelt upon the corporate virtues which only in part depend upon the material associations of this famous place, and yet it is that corporate feeling which more and more seems to me to be the essential virtue of this institution; something inseparably associated, I agree, with the chapel, the playing fields, the school yard, the river—all the material facts with which we are so familiar.

There is something behind that corporate feeling which unites Etonians. Wherever they find themselves, in any part of the world, engaged in some great labour, some great conflict, it may be suffering under some great stress, then, irrespective of age, irrespective of occupation, the man feels those with whom he is working are Etonians, and the very fact that they are Eton men gives him a confidence without further question or inquiry which he could hardly feel with regard to those brought up under different and, as we Etonians are vain enough to think, less fortunate circumstances.

On this day last year I was one of the British delegates in Paris dealing with the tremendous problems of peace. We decided that the day should not pass without celebrating our ancient school, and a goodly number met together in Paris—Paris secure by that time from air raids and long-distance guns, Paris engaged in framing to the best of its ability the new framework of Europe.

We were drawn from all occupations. There

were soldiers, there were sailors, diplomatists, lawyers, experts in all the spheres of administration. Two of us, I remember, were Americans, attached to the American Mission in Paris, but Etonians loyal to the backbone, and there we met together and celebrated our old school.

I am told that similar scenes took place within the hearing of the German guns at the front, when this anniversary came round in circumstances of great anxiety and peril. Then Etonians of all military ranks met together and celebrated their old school, sent cheerful challenges to their hereditary enemy—I do not refer to the Germans—I refer to the Harrovians—and felt that even in the imminent perils of war they gained strength and cheerfulness and courage from the consciousness of the memory that all held in common, and the inspiration which they brought from their early education within these walls.

It is a wonderful thing that such an institution should have grown up, and no man has yet been able to explain the secret of its growth. Like all that is best in this country, it is what it is by a process of development, difficult to explain, difficult to describe, not easy even mentally to grasp, but clear to every man who has eyes to see and ears to hear, and that power of sympathetic imagination which enables him to understand what are the realities behind the shows of life.

That I should be thought worthy by representatives of Eton to have my portrait placed amongst those here, all men of mark and note, is an honour which I shall not and cannot forget and which I cannot easily exaggerate even if I have not deserved—and I fear I have not—all the things which Lord Curzon and Lord Dartmouth have been good enough to say of me. They have not exaggerated what I owe to the school. They have not exaggerated the affection in which I hold it, and they cannot possibly exaggerate the feelings of gratitude with which I accept this great honour now, as my career is drawing to a close.

## 4

### On Memories of Parliament

*Speech at a Dinner in the Grocers' Hall given by the City of London Conservative and Unionist Association, June 20th, 1922*

I HAVE now been in public life for nearly half a century. It is a long vista to look back upon, and I cannot help reflecting what great dramas have been begun, continued, and ended within my own recollection and my own direct experience.

When I think of domestic affairs in the House of Commons, which have been so long the central preoccupation of my life, I recall that I have seen the rise, the culmination, and the decline, of that most marvellous parliamentary phenomenon, the Irish Party under Mr. Parnell. I do not know what the future historian will say about that party; I would like to instruct him, and if he were to read my words he might be sure that I am giving him a correct picture from the point of view from which I am now speaking. I do not believe that in the whole history of our, or perhaps of any other Parliament, there has ever been such a party, for the sternness of its discipline, the extraordinary wealth of admirable speakers it contained, some of them great masters of elocution and admirable debaters, formidable from their knowledge of Parliamentary methods, and the use to which they put that knowledge. We Britons often thought it misuse, but now I speak impersonally, politics apart. In regard to the use to which those men put that knowledge I do not believe there has ever been so remarkable a party as the Irish Party. I saw its rise and its small beginnings in the first Parliament of which I was a member, and I saw it when Parnell took the leadership, and I saw its culmination and its decline.

So much for domestic politics. That was one great drama of which I have seen all stages. I also saw another great drama touching infinitely greater interests. I accompanied Lord Salisbury, my uncle, when he went to Paris in the first train that entered the French capital after the Commune was defeated in 1871, only a few weeks after the King of Prussia had been declared Emperor of Germany in the Palace of Versailles. I was a young man then, but I was within three years of becoming a Member of Parliament. I went then in a humble capacity when Germany had the unquestioned leadership of Europe, and I have lived to sign on behalf of my country as Foreign Minister, in the great gallery where the Emperor William first became Emperor, the Treaty of Versailles that ended the Empire to whose beginnings I have referred.

These were two great dramas, and if I look back upon those long years that have elapsed since 1874 I have thoughts of the long procession of great and

distinguished Parliament figures that have crossed
the stage since that time. I saw Mr. Disraeli
and Mr. Gladstone in the House of Commons,
each the adored leader of his party, and I have
seen all their successors. Among them were
men of great gifts and great service, occupying on
one side or the other places in the State, but whose
names are perhaps scarcely known to the rising generation, although they filled the newspapers of their
day.

The history of the British House of Commons is
a wonderful history. This long succession which
falls within my memory, and the immemorial line
of their predecessors going back into the remotest
history, forms a galaxy of political talent which
has not only made the British Empire what it is,
but has made it the model on which those who seek
freedom combined with order, endeavour, directly or
indirectly, to frame their institutions. Do not let us
fear that the future is going to be less glorious than
the past. I proclaim myself an optimist. All of us in
this room, the youngest and the oldest, have recently
lived through years which might try our optimism
to the utmost, but I beg you not to let it fail. We
are not less capable of sustaining the burden of
Empire than were our fathers before us. The task
is now one of great difficulty. Problems of which
in our youth and even in our maturity we never
dreamt seem to multiply upon us, until those who
endeavour to see the way through the immediate
future are almost overwhelmed with the number
and the magnitude of the questions with which they

have to deal.   But let us not lose faith or courage.
For my own part, my share in carrying on public
business is inevitably near its close.   But I look
forward with unflinching faith to the success of the
labours of those who are going to follow the generation to which I belong, and the generation which
it succeeded, for I know that you will not fall short
of the example which we have endeavoured to set
you, and which our fathers before us have set.

   To be an optimist is to be a believer in youth.
It is, after all, the young people who are going
to do this work.   Let us believe in them.   I believe
in them.   Doubtless they occasionally have their
weaknesses.   And among these weaknesses sometimes is a very imperfect appreciation of the virtues
of their seniors.   But these weaknesses are always
amiable; they always give me at least a great feeling
of pleasure mixed with a slight touch of pathos.
When I hear of the new art I know it is going to be
the old art quite soon.   When I hear that there is
going to be a new school of politics I know that in
a year or two its professors will be described as
"the old gang."   That, after all, is how the world
is made, and, after all, it is not a bad way.   If it
were not for the young how would the world move?
Whatever the old people may think of themselves,
it is inevitable that they should be somewhat petrified by long experience as well as taught by it, and
that they should lose some of that flexibility of mind
which is possessed by youth.

## 5
## On War Memories

*Speech at the Unveiling of the War Memorial in Whittingehame Parish*

I AM deeply grateful for the opportunity which has been given me to take part in this most touching and moving ceremony. Unfortunately I am rarely master of my own movements, and those who had the organisation of this gathering have kindly arranged it so that I should be able to take part.

I see before me representatives from the whole parish. Two absences there are which personally come home to me. That is of my two nephews, Frank and Oswald, known to all of you brought up here, and who in the Great War bore their share of wounds and of dangers. Unfortunately wide seas separate us now. They are serving their country far from this scene, and though I doubt not that their thoughts are with us, we are denied their bodily presence. Others there are doubtless, of whom I have heard nothing, who are prevented from being here and taking their part in the ceremony, but I would fain hope that not only all the relations of those whose greatness and fame we are here commemorating, but also those who were their brothers-in-arms during the war, have found it possible to be present.

Is it not an occasion which necessarily and deeply moves us to the very centre of our being? All of you have read accounts of the more than regal ceremonies which attended the sepulture in Westminster Abbey of the Unknown Warrior. Unknown indeed he is, but the nation took him as a symbol of all who had perished in the great cause by land or sea, and round his remains, and in the ceremony by which the sepulture was accompanied, all Britain expressed symbolically what was felt with regard to those who had sacrificed their lives in the cause of their country.

Here we are met together with something of a more personal note. It is not an unknown warrior that we have met here to commemorate; it is those who were known to all of us, who moved in our midst, were our friends or our acquaintances, and who left at one period or another of the Great War —many of them very early in the day, perceiving by a kind of intuition the great services that were required of them. It is for them, and, as it were, in their personal honour, that we are met here to-day, and here we welcome those, their own relatives, who suffered irreparable loss when they were taken away, but who, at all events, have the consolation of knowing that their names will be recorded, and are recorded in history, and that their neighbours have shown their deep recognition of all that they did for their country and for us, by erecting this memorial in their honour.

Time, I trust, has softened the inevitable misery of separation, but no time can efface the outlines or dim the writing which records that their sons or their brothers have earned for themselves the un-dying gratitude of those who knew them best.

This is a personal memorial. It is a memorial given by their neighbours to those whom they knew personally and individually, but, believe me, it has a wider reference, a more extended significance. None of us standing here—scarcely even the children whose memories must be a little faint about what occurred even three or four years ago—are likely ever to have effaced from our memories the trials, the dangers, the anxieties, the defeats, the victories, and the final triumph of the greatest of all wars.

Which of us is likely to underrate the share which Scotland has borne, with the whole of Britain, and with the whole of the British Empire, in the great struggle which came to an end on November 11th, 1918? Which of us, reading these names, can ever have obliterated from our minds the long stories of the hardship and triumphs of the armies in France, the more distant glories of Meso-potamia, all that was suffered, all that was lost, and let me add, all that was gained, by the sacri-fices at the Dardanelles, all that the British Fleet did to sustain the Allied cause? None of us are likely to forget it. None of us, at all events, living, as we do, in sight of the Firth of Forth, are likely to doubt what history will inevitably and amply prove—the great thesis that it was the British Navy which made the victory of the British Army and the Allied Armies possible, and it was upon that unshakable foundation that the whole victory of the Allies rested.

That is the broad way in which we, who have lived through those eventful years, look at it. As time goes on, as those who took part, either as spectators or actors, in the great drama, one by one are removed from the scene, no doubt these memorials will have their outline somewhat softened, the sharpness of recollection will vanish, and those great things will fall into the charge of the historian. Do not suppose that when that time comes the value of this memorial will be otherwise than increased. We do not require a memorial to keep us in mind of the devoted men who have sacrificed their lives for us, but when we are gone and when strangers pass along that road, seeing this monument and reading the names recorded thereon, they will say to themselves one of two things.

I know not what the state of the world will be when the period that I am speaking of comes upon us, but if our most sanguine hopes are fulfilled, and if the strenuous labours and unfaltering faith of men of goodwill really do contrive to introduce some less barbarous method of dealing with international disputes than international butchery, then the traveller will say, looking at this monument, "These are the names of men who by fighting and suffering and losing their lives in this greatest of all wars have given us and the world perpetual peace." May that happen!

I am one of the sanguine ones. I am one of those who think that as civilisation advances it will become more and more intolerable that the world should go through from time to time anything like the agonies from which we have just issued. But supposing that in my sanguine moments I am deceived, as well I may be. Then will this monument have lost its value, will its moral be deprived of its essential point? Believe me, no. If it so happens that the infamous passion for domination which was the cause of this war, and which for the moment we stamped out, should again threaten the peace and liberties of the world, if again we, or our children, our grandchildren, or our great-grandchildren, are threatened by a renewal of the horrors from which we have escaped, then men will turn to monuments like this, and will say, "In the time of our fathers or grandfathers all the greatest interests of humanity hung for a time suspended in the balance. Then they showed of what metal they were made; they came forward and threw back the wave of invasion which was likely to overwhelm all that was most valued." And men will say to themselves, "If a like trial comes upon us, if we in our turn have to sacrifice ourselves for a great cause, shall we do less than those whose immortal memory is preserved upon this monument?"

May this monument which I have just unveiled remain for all time as a record of what the men in this parish could do and did in the greatest crisis in the world's history.

# 6

## ON THE PRESS GALLERY

*Speech at the Annual Dinner of the Members of the Parliamentary Press Gallery, April 11th, 1908*

I THINK any politician who is the guest of such a company as that which I see assembled before me must necessarily come before them with some feelings of diffidence; not because he has nothing surprising in the way of oratory to give them—they must be sick to death of his methods. (Cries of "Not of yours.")

At all events, he has nothing new to tell them as his methods of speech or as to his powers of stringing words together. My diffidence, at any rate, is dissipated both by the kindness of such interruptions as that which has been courteously made, and by the two speeches which have been made this evening. The first speaker narrated an anecdote, the substance of which, I confess, I had forgotten. The general purport of it was that any person connected with our leading newspapers who calls upon me at 1 a.m. for the purpose of obtaining important news in an interesting national crisis, may find me in my dressing-gown and slippers, courteous and communicative.

I hope I shall always be both courteous and

communicative as far as public interests permit. I am grateful to Mr. Peacock for his recollections; and for the very flattering manner in which he has narrated the anecdote; which, I may say without vanity, does credit to both of us. At the same time, may I, humbly and respectfully, put in a plea that everybody who wants information will choose the hours between 12 noon and 12 midnight, rather than the hours between 12 midnight and 12 noon, in which to see me?

As for the speech in which Mr. Hughes proposed my health, I have again nothing but thanks. He was more than kind in his reference to myself. He told me that I provide the raw material for the manufacture of a large amount of goods which go about the country in the daily Press, and, at any rate, whatever our fiscal views may be, none of us desire to put a tax on raw material.

I have nothing to complain of, very much the contrary, as to the way in which this particular raw material is worked up for public use. Like other politicians, I have those who criticise my views, those who applaud them, those who understand them, and those who explain them. I have no quarrel with any of these various classes of commentators except perhaps the last. I am sure I am always more or less happy when I am being praised, and not very uncomfortable when I am being abused; but I have moments of uneasiness when I am being explained. But that I suppose is common to all mankind. We all of us like to explain ourselves, and we are all of us equally resentful when there are people so extraordinarily perverse that they do not understand our views. I have greatly suffered in that way; but I do not know that I have suffered more than my species generally, and I bear my sufferings, I hope, with adequate philosophy.

Mr. Hughes also referred to a speech of mine in which my opinion on holidays was referred to. I had forgotten that statement, but it is my good fortune to be a consistent thinker, and, therefore, I am never dismayed or embarrassed when previous utterances of mine are referred to. Mr. Hughes said the opinion I expressed was that holidays should begin early and last long. That reference to my opinion is a happy illustration of that consistency between a politician's opinion when he is in office, and a politician's opinion when he is in opposition, which might be a model to all my kind.

I do not know whether I ought to say anything with regard to that part of the proposer's speech which referred to the other guests who are present here. There is the chairman of the Kitchen Committee, a very old Parliamentary friend of mine. He watches over our material interests, and no doubt, under his guidance and that of his predecessors', the well-being of all those who are connected with the work of the House of Commons is admirably looked after. It was apparently well looked after in earlier days. I read a story to-day of a distinguished gentleman who reported in the Press Gallery just about 100 years ago. He had not the advantages we now possess, but he had dined well at Bellamy's,

and he came into the gallery of the House of Commons having had an excellent dinner, washed down
with excellent wine. He was bored with the debate
—I imagine many gentlemen here are bored with
the debate. (A voice, "Not when you are speaking.") He was wearied with the superfluity of
rhetoric, which, in spite of what pessimistic critics
say, prevailed quite as much 100 years ago as it
does now. At any rate, getting bored, he asked the
Speaker for a song. The anecdote is, I believe, perfectly true, and it derives a great deal of humour
from the fact that the Speaker was Mr. Addington,
a gentleman who was nothing if not proper. The
whole House, except the Speaker, was convulsed
with laughter. The Serjeant-at-Arms was appealed
to. He went to the gallery, and he inquired for the
culprit. The culprit retained the presence of mind
to point to a respectable Quaker sitting below him,
and this gentleman was actually taken into custody
as the author of the outrage.

If I may say so that is an anecdote which the
chairman of the Kitchen Committee should take to
heart. He should remember that we have to be
careful in these matters, and that, in spite of the
happy increase of temperance in the last 100 years,
it would be very unfortunate if Mr. Speaker were
now asked for a song, great as is the difference
between the present occupier of the chair and the
respectable gentleman who occupied it 100 years
ago.

I do not think it would be proper that I should
terminate a speech of thanks in reply to this toast

without saying, on behalf of all the members of the House of Commons present and absent, how much we recognise what we owe to those who watch and report our proceedings. There may be some kind of collision of interest. The man who did more than anyone else to promote Parliamentary reporting about 100 years ago is said to have summarised his opinion in this short sentence: "The members of the House of Commons never thought the reports of their speeches too long, and the public never thought them too short." There is, no doubt, that perennial difference of opinion between the makers of speeches and those who first report and then print them. Nevertheless, although reporting is contrary to all the standing orders of the House, and is a gross breach of our privileges, it must be admitted that the reporting has been, and is, admirably done in this country.

In the first place, it is, as far as I know, absolutely impartial. I do not say that of the accounts of the debates. I think, if you compare the general conspectus, the general picture, of a debate drawn in one journal with that in another of a different political complexion, you will probably find some difficulty in reconciling conflicting views. But the reporting of what is actually said is, I believe, absolutely impartial and excellent. Moreover, most of us who have to make speeches—and I am told that, judged by the number of columns, I make more speeches than anybody else in the House of Commons —suspect that the speaker owes more to the reporter than, perhaps, we are always prepared to admit.

I do not go to the length of saying that all the good things are put into a speech which the speaker never uttered, though that has been done. Lord Brougham is said to have republished a speech of his into which the reporter had put a good many quotations from Cicero. I give public notice that if any speech of mine appears with Latin quotations in it, those quotations are due to the reporter, and are not due to me. At all events, the classic languages apart, we all of us owe to the kind attention of the reporter the excision of many superfluities, not always, perhaps, regarded as superfluities by the orator, the correction of many gross errors of grammar, and an improvement to our oratory which we may be reluctant to admit, but which is nevertheless there. In the name, therefore, not only of your guests this evening, but of that large body of loquacious gentlemen, of which it appears I am the most loquacious, I beg to tender to this Society my warm thanks, not merely for the hospitality which we have received from you this evening, but for the work which you have done to improve our oratory, to spread our opinions, and to make clear the opinions which we conceive, at any rate, that we hold. From all these points of view, and in all these capacities, I beg to thank you, gentlemen, most warmly and most heartily for your hospitality this evening.

## 7

### ON LISTER, PASTEUR AND SIMPSON

*Speech at the Lister Centenary Celebration, Edinburgh, July 20th, 1927*

THE Medical Association surely could not meet in Edinburgh on the centenary of Lister's birth without calling together an assembly such as this to do him honour.  Lister was not indeed born north of the Tweed, but it was in Scotland that he matured his great discoveries.  It was in two Scottish Universities that he made his fame, or if that is too strong a phrase, that he laid the solid foundations of his immortal fame.  It was to Edinburgh, both in the earlier part and in the latter part of his Scottish career, that he always turned with affectionate regard, and never, to the end of his life, did he fail in his affection for his colleagues, and for the University to which he added such lustre, and which had given him his opportunities.

Lister was a very great man, but, like every other great man, he owed part of his greatness to the fact that the moment at which his career began was a moment at which his peculiar and special gifts found their peculiar and their special opportunity. That he would have been a great surgeon at any period of the world's history, that he would have added lustre to the pursuit of medicine wherever he had been born, I do not doubt. That he was enabled to write his name in indelible characters upon the history of medicine was largely due to the fact that he was the contemporary of two very great men—Simpson and Pasteur. Pasteur's position in the history of civilisation is fixed and immortal. It is impossible to estimate the services and the position which Lister occupied in the history of surgery without remembering their relation to that discovery of chloroform which we owe to Simpson, and without which it would be impossible to perform, even under the most perfect aseptic conditions, the operations which have added so greatly to our knowledge of diseases, and diminished so greatly the sufferings of mankind. The two discoveries mutually assisted one another.

Surgery without aseptic treatment was too often the harbinger of death rather than the cause of health and recovery. Therefore, when we think of the joint services of all those great men, we should remember the character of the double debt which we owe them. It is not merely the debt of individual patients to the skilled physician who has healed our wounds. It is the debt which we owe to the growth of knowledge. That debt is not merely a debt to the ingenious and skilful surgeon, the inventor of this or that mode of dressing wounds, nor yet to the inventive and bold experiments of men like Sir James Simpson. It is the combination of the two on which I would like those who are interested in the progress of knowledge to fix their attention, and to recognise that without both the great men who co-operated in this result, the result itself could hardly have occurred.  It was the skill with which Lister seized on Pasteur's discovery, and saw in that discovery the key to the problem on which his mind had been fixedly set year after year; it is the effect which all this has had upon the pain, the suffering, of the most suffering classes of the community, the classes of the invalid, the victims of accidents, all those who suffer from painful, agonising, often fatal diseases, it is the effect upon their destiny which has brought together this great multitude which I see before me.

It is a terrible page in the history of medicine to read what went on under the almost agonised eyes of the surgeons themselves in the best hospitals, in the greatest capitals of Europe and America.  It makes one's blood almost run cold.  In the centenary volume in honour of Lister which has just been published there is one terrible sentence.  I confess I can hardly think of it now without emotion.  It seems there was in a hospital, I think, in Vienna, one ward, which had so awful a reputation for the fatal effects on the unhappy patients, that women used to implore with tears that to that death-trap they should not be sent.  Let us conceive a situation of that kind—horrible to the surgeons, horrible, though fortunately not always known, to the patients, the very story of which makes one feel that, of all the benefactors of suffering and sick mankind, the greatest benefactor of all was Lister himself.

I own to some surprise that Lister's discoveries were not immediately hailed by the whole profession with the approval which now universally meets them. It is very easy to be wise after the event, and nobody need boast of possessing that facile form of wisdom. But look at it as I may, I am still profoundly puzzled at the first reception that Lister's discovery got from his colleagues. In no place—even including Glasgow and Edinburgh —was it received with that universal acclaim of approval which one would have supposed would have greeted a remedy for what everybody admitted to be almost a scandal to the medical profession.

After all, these experiments of Lister were not laboratory experiments carried on in some unknown centre of learning. They were not couched in unknown tongues. They were not taught in unknown schools. The very surgeons who refused to accept with enthusiasm, and to aid with their approval, the new movement, lived in the same building. They had the full opportunity of seeing the effects, and, yet, for some reason quite unintelligible, they remained unconverted. After all, putrefaction was a very obvious phenomenon, and if they could see by walking across a passage that in one ward putrefaction prevailed with all its disastrous and horrible consequences, and that in another it did not prevail, I would have thought that was an experience which every man of science and common sense would have accepted.

I hesitate to express any condemnation of that

frame of mind when I remember that Sir James Simpson was himself one of the doubters. Of that great man I would never speak without profound reverence. I knew him as a youngster, and I received many kindnesses from him, who was one of the most lovable of men. It is a strange fact that Simpson had been one of the most eloquent exponents of all the horrors attending surgery at that date, yet he died in 1870—in the early days of the Listerian regime—unconverted to the process. I wish that Simpson had survived even a few years. I wish he could have been here to-day, because I am sure that great man would have been the first, and the most eloquent, and the most sincere, of those who felt that the great addition Lister made to Simpson's own discovery of anæsthetics was one which would bring them joined together in a common fame.

These memorials or centenaries of great men are increasing phenomena, and, I think, good ones. I have myself been concerned within relatively a few months in at least six—Bacon, Newton, Farraday, Beethoven, Richard Bright, and now, to-day, Lister—a great catalogue of great names. The services which these men have rendered to mankind cannot be weighed and cannot be compared. We only know they are beyond estimate and outside all machinery for comparative valuation, yet I would venture to say that even in that splendid catalogue the name of Lister stands out supreme in this respect—that, by his forethought, his determination to reach that certain goal, the inspiration of genius which enabled him to grasp at once the full significance of Pasteur's discovery, he, of all these names, had the inestimable blessing of having by his efforts immediately and directly diminished, to an extent quite incalculable, the sufferings of mankind. That is surely the most glorious tribute we can pay to any man, and I rejoice to think that Lister lived long enough to be able to see the full value of his own work, and left to those who survive him a debt of gratitude which they can never pay, and which in succeeding generations will only accumulate.

SECTION II
A POLITICAL MISCELLANY

# I

## ON NATIONALISM, CHIEFLY SCOTTISH

*Speech at the 248th St. Andrew's Day Festival of
the Royal Scottish Corporation, 19th November, 1912*

I RISE to propose the toast of the evening—
prosperity to this great and ancient Corporation.
The value of its services are acknowledged by all
who have watched its work, and by all who know
what it has done for our countrymen whom misfortune, deserved or undeserved, may have left
stranded in this great Metropolis. But it has a
claim upon our affection and regard far beyond
the limits of its beneficent work in this year or that
year of its existence.

We date practically from the time when the
Crown of Scotland and the Crown of England were
first placed upon the same head; from the time when
the Union was begun, and legally brought to its
full perfection, some little more than two centuries
ago—the Union which has been growing in strength,
bearing from day to day better fruits since those
early days in which it was begun. It is hard for
us to put ourselves in the position of a Scotsman
coming in the train of James the Sixth of Scotland
and the First of England, and seeking his fortunes

in the southern part of these islands. He no doubt spoke the same speech; no doubt the literature of Scotland can never be considered apart from the literature of England, go back as far as you will. But yet the two countries through an unhappy fate had not only been separated, but had been antagonistic for centuries before, and the memory, the greatest patriotic memory of every Scotsman, went back to the time when he was fighting his English brother. Whatever England did, Scotland, from the very necessities of her then political situation, did the very opposite, and could not do otherwise, and these memories, which, remember, to us are mere history, to the Scotsmen who came south when this great Corporation was first begun were living memories. They were memories of which they themselves may have had experience, in regard to which their fathers, grandfathers, great-grandfathers, back for many generations would have supplied them with endless tales of feuds, rivalries, bloody combats, hostile diplomacy, endless wars. No wonder that the Scotsman felt himself a stranger in the southern land; and that feeling naturally went on for many years after the union of the Crowns, and for not a few years after the union of the countries. You will find it in all literature, and the position, no doubt even after the Union, of a Scotsman coming to London, entering Parliament, and taking his place in the great Imperial interests of the country, was not always an easy one. Although he spoke the same language, he did not speak with the same accent.

It is an interesting reflection that some of the greatest debaters in the eighteenth century in the British House of Commons were Scotsmen—like Wedderburn, who had deliberately and laboriously to modify his ancestral method of speech so as to make himself a great power, as he did, both in the House of Commons and in the Law Courts. And David Hume, one of the greatest writers—I do not talk of his philosophy, it is not an after-dinner subject—that we the British have produced, you will find, if you look at a complete edition of his works, a list of the Scotticisms that he had laboriously to avoid in order to write the language in the classical style which he made his own.

These were not small difficulties. They were great difficulties and, if time has entirely abolished them, remember that time has done it gradually, and that no great fusion, political or any other, can be done by a stroke of the pen. If it is to be permanent as ours is permanent, it must be a work of much preliminary toil, many misunderstandings, some difficulties, some frictions, and when those difficulties and frictions are got over, the welding in that furnace cannot be unloosened, and what has been joined together never can again be separated.

I do not want as a Scotsman among Scotsmen to spend too much time in praising ourselves. In the first place, I think, in the opinion of most Scotsmen, it is an unnecessary operation. We have got that kind of unassailable self-content which makes us perfectly indifferent to hostile criticism. We pity our critics, but we do not think it neces-

sary to be angry.   Yet there is one praise which I
hope I may be permitted to give to our own country, and it is this.   I think we really have, beyond
all the world, set an example how to reconcile naturally and completely, and without effort, two things
which at first do not seem easily reconciled.    I
mean the intense and ardent patriotism for a part,
which yet only reinforces and strengthens the larger
patriotism for the whole.   Believe me, this possibility is of more importance than at first sight
appears.   The doctrine of nationality, which has
played so great and so beneficent a part in the
construction and reconstruction of the modern
world, has been a great engine for uniting sections
of the Empire.   Occasionally, here and there, it
has had the opposite and ill consequence of dividing men.   We Scotsmen—I do not think I am over-
praising ourselves—have seen how to reconcile the
principle and feeling of nationality, the consciousness of a separate history in many respects, during
many formative and important centuries, and how
to do this without feeling that there was any antagonism whatever for that patriotism, not more
ardent, indeed, but larger in scope, which includes
Great Britain, and not Great Britain alone, but the
whole Empire of which we are citizens.

It is only by following the example that we have
set that the future of the Empire can be made
absolutely secure.   The Canadian, the Australian,
the New Zealander, they must have, and they ought
to have, and they will have, their own feeling of
separate nationality.   The Canadian is a Canadian.

He wants, and he ought to want, to feel that Canada has got its own principles of development, its own future; so also has the Australian, pursuing the great experiments of freedom and self-government on very different lines from those of Canada, lines which Australia has chosen for herself as a free country, and as a member of that great congeries of free countries which make up our Empire. Do not let us discourage their feeling of local patriotism. Let us only ask them to follow the example of Scotland and to cultivate that feeling of nationality for themselves—Canada for the Canadians, Australia for the Australians, and all for the British Empire. It was because this conception was new in the history of the world, was not understood, and, let us in fairness remember, could not be understood, by our forefathers one hundred and fifty years ago, that the great and unhappy division between us and our American colonies took place. It perhaps required that great lesson to teach us what we now know. We have learned the lesson, and, following the lead of Scotland, the British Empire is showing how to work these two apparently antagonistic principles so that even those who praise them both never even see that there can possibly be any inconsistency between them.

Let me return to what ought to have been, and was, my proper subject, which is the help which Scotsmen outside Scotland can give to their fellow-countrymen whose lot has fallen upon evil days. We have in our own country quarrelled quite enough, perhaps, about politics; we have quarrelled perhaps a little more than enough about matters theological and ecclesiastical, but quarrel as we may at home, we always remember that though we are not in Scotland we are all Scotsmen, and that whatever be the differences of sect or creed or political opinion, the fact that a man is a Scotsman is by itself a claim for the kindness and the charity and help of every Scotsman. It is upon that foundation that this Corporation is based. It is upon that foundation that it has lasted for all these generations. I see this is described as the two hundred and forty-eighth ceremony of this kind. Long may these sentiments flourish among our countrymen. Long may this Corporation carry out that beneficent work in the future which it has so admirably and so successfully performed in the past.

## On Nationality and Home Rule*

*Based upon a Speech delivered in Nottingham in 1913. Afterwards published as an Article in the University Magazine, Montreal, in October, 1913, and reprinted as a Pamphlet by Messrs. Longman, Green & Co. in the same year*

Is THERE an Irish problem? If there be an Irish problem, what is its character and what is its origin? Can the Home Rule Bill now before Parliament do anything substantial towards its solution? These are the questions which every citizen of the United Kingdom, and, in a less degree, every citizen of the Empire, is bound to ask; for on the answers given must depend the immediate future of the country. The subject is so complex that it cannot be embraced within the limits of a brief article like the present. It is so controversial that an impartial treatment of it is almost beyond the reach of human endeavour. Yet there are one or two broad issues on which even now it may be worth while to say something; for in the heat of debate and the clash of disputes aroused by minor issues they are apt to be forgotten or ignored.

The first question of those which I began by

---

*Corrected by Lord Balfour.

asking must without doubt be answered in the affirmative. There *is* an Irish problem. Its gravity may be a matter of dispute, but its reality is beyond question. But what exactly is its character, and how has it arisen? Evidently we have not here to do with the ordinary case—familiar enough in history—of a down-trodden nationality. Ireland is neither robbed nor oppressed. It is not exploited in the interests of British financiers or of British taxpayers. If there is exploiting, it is the other way. Far from Ireland not having its fair share in the councils of the United Kingdom, it has far more than its fair share. It sends more than its proportionate number of representatives to the British Parliament, as is admitted by everybody, including the authors of the Home Rule Bill. But, in addition to this, it has in every English and Scottish city an important section of the population who vote avowedly and openly as Irishmen, in favour of the candidate indicated by Nationalist Whips and supporting the policy of Nationalist leaders. I do not complain—far from it; I merely insist that no Irishman, wherever he lives, who knows the circumstances of this country, who knows the conditions under which members are sent to Westminster to represent the people of the United Kingdom, will for one instant pretend that Ireland has not her share, and more than her share, of parliamentary power. If, therefore, Ireland has a national grievance, it is one of a somewhat unusual type. She is in the position, singular among "oppressed" nationalities, of enjoying more than her fair proportion of representation in the Imperial Parliament, and paying less than her fair proportion of taxation to Imperial objects.

If, then, we want to find the justification for Home Rule, we must look elsewhere. We shall never find it either in the existing parliamentary system or in the existing financial system. There, if there *be* grievances, they are British, not Irish. Where, then, lies the Irish difficulty? English supporters of Home Rule give us scant information on this point. They talk about the congestion of parliamentary business. They talk about the embarrassments which the Irish question has caused to successive governments. There *is* congestion; and there *are* embarrassments; but they do not constitute the Irish question. The difficulty does not lie there, and everybody who takes the trouble to inquire may easily convince himself that it does not lie there. Where does it lie? It lies in the fact that the Irish Nationalist party claim that Ireland, *on the ground of her separate nationality,* possesses inherent rights which cannot be satisfied by the fairest and fullest share in the parliamentary institutions of the United Kingdom. What is enough for Scotsmen and Englishmen can never be enough for them. To think so would be treason to Ireland.

The sentiment of nationality is one of a group of such sentiments for which there is unfortunately no common name. Loyalties to a country, a party, a constitution, a national sovereign, a tribal chief, a church, a race, a creed, are characteristic speci-

mens of the class. They may be ill-directed, they
often are. Nevertheless it is such loyalties that
make human society possible; they do more, they
make it noble. To them we owe it that a man will
sacrifice ease, profit, life itself, for something which
wholly transcends his merely personal interests.
Therefore, whether mistaken or not, there is always
in them a touch of greatness; and were I so extreme
a Unionist as to think that an Irishman should
cherish no special sentiment for the part of the
United Kingdom wherein he was born—and I
think exactly the reverse—I should still regard his
feelings of patriotism, however narrow, as worthy
of respect.

But it has to be observed that the kind of
loyalty we call patriotism, though it expresses a
simple feeling, need have no exclusive application.
It may embrace a great deal more than a man's
country or a man's race. It may embrace a great
deal less. And these various patriotisms need not
be, and should not be, mutually exclusive. As
civilisation advances, it becomes more and more
necessary for men to learn how loyalties are to be
combined without being weakened; how a narrow
provincialism is to be avoided on the one side, and
a selfish indifference, masquerading under the name
of enlightened cosmopolitanism, is to be shunned on
the other.

As a matter of fact, some combination of different patriotisms is almost universal among thinking
persons. If I consider the case I know best
(namely, my own), I find that, within a general

regard for mankind, which I hope is not absent nor weak, I am moved by a feeling, especially patriotic in its character, for the group of nations who are the authors and the guardians of western civilisation, for the sub-group which speaks the English language, and whose laws and institutions are rooted in British history, for the communities which compose the British Empire, for the United Kingdom of which I am a citizen, and for Scotland, where I was born, and which is my home, as it was the home of my fathers before me. If patriotisms such as these are not forced into antagonism, they may not only be consistent with each other, but they may mutually reinforce each other; and statesmanship can have no higher aim than to make harmony between them easy, and conflict impossible.

It is easy to see, even from this very summary statement, how various are the centres round which patriotic sentiment may crystallise. Its occasion may be found in a real or supposed community of race, of language, of religion, of institutions, of culture. It may be due to geographical conditions; or it may be the offspring of common memories, or of common hopes, or of common material or political interests. Only of this we may be sure, that whatever its origin in the past or justification in the present, it will not be content with these. It will draw without scruple nourishment from every source, and if history prove insufficient legend will fill the gap.

Now what is there in the character of Irish

patriotism which, in the case of the southern and western portions of the Island, produces or keeps alive the desire to break up the Union? It is not the sense of present grievance, either agrarian, financial, or administrative. The agrarian difficulty is in the way of solution under the Wyndham (and other) Acts: the financial position is more favourable to Ireland than to Great Britain; the administrative grievance is largely imaginary. What then is it?

Judging by Nationalist speeches you might suppose that it was the destruction by England of Irish institutions, built up by the labours of an Irish race, and giving political unity to an Irish nation. On this theory Ireland is a kind of Poland, deprived by stronger neighbours of its constitution and its independence: so that the proper remedy is now to undo this ancient wrong, and restore to the Irish people the national glories of which they should never have been deprived.

I believe this view, held more or less explicitly by most Irishmen of Nationalist leaning throughout the world and by many who are not Irishmen, is at the root of all the sentiment which has lain behind the Home Rule propaganda from the days of O'Connell to the present moment. But in truth it is a complete delusion. The history on which it is based is imaginary history. Ireland has often in centuries gone by been hardly used by her more powerful neighbours. But she has never been deprived of her national organisation, for she never possessed one. Ask an Irish Nation-

alist what ancient institution he desires to see restored to his native country. If he replies at all,
the institution he names will certainly prove to be
of English origin, and to have been abolished because it failed. Nor is the case different with
literature, or law, or parliamentary eloquence. In
all these great departments of human activity men
born in Ireland have done splendid work. But it
has been in adding to the masterpieces of English
literature, in moulding or administering English
law, in adorning assemblies of English origin.

And mark well that this is no fault of the Irish,
or, for that matter, of the English either. It is
due to the historic accident that the first effective
contact between England and Ireland took place
at a period when the political system of the former,
backward as we rightly deem it, was yet incomparably superior to the tribal organisation which
still prevailed in Ireland. So at least I interpret
the course of events; but whether I be right or
wrong, this, at least, is certain, that the English
invader, whatever his crimes, found nothing and
destroyed nothing in the Ireland of the twelfth (or
later) centuries which could by any possibility be
restored to the Ireland of the twentieth.

But granting, it may be replied, that Nationalist
hostility to the Union or to Britain cannot be
justified on the ground that Britain has destroyed
an Irish civilisation, may it not find a surer base
in the opinion that the Union yokes together men
of different race in one artificial and unworkable
system? And is not the system unworkable

because the men that have to work it *are* of different race?

On this question of race there seems to me much exaggeration and error. We who live now in the United Kingdom, or whose fathers emigrated thence to the new countries of the West, are doubtless of mixed descent, and doubtless the mixture is variously compounded in different districts. But there is not, so far as I know, the slightest reason for supposing that the difference is greater between Ireland and Great Britain than between parts of England and Wales, or between the Highlands of Scotland and the Lowlands. Indeed if any doctrinaire is going to preach the reconstitution of the United Kingdom on the basis of anthropology, he will never be content with the simple plan of Home Rule all round. He would among other small changes have to move the south-east frontier of Scotland far to the north, and its south-west frontier far to the south of their present position; a proceeding to which I for one would most strongly object. If race and blood be the essential root of Nationalist theories as applied to the United Kingdom, the Scotland of history must perish, and Ulster must be divided from the rest of Ireland.

If then neither Irish institutions, nor Irish culture, nor Irish descent be a sufficient ground for the claim of Home Rule, can we find that ground in its geographical isolation? It is a perilous argument; for geographical isolation is at the mercy of mechanical knowledge; and it changes with the progress of invention under our very eyes. If anything is certain in hypothetical history it is that there never would have been a separate Parliament on College Green had Dublin always been within ten hours of London. I quite understand that a system of subordinate provinces may be convenient in a country of vast area and scattered populations. But to acknowledge separate nationality, or even to create a separate administration, in a district which is neither remote nor difficult of access, for no other reason than that it is surrounded by water, seems to be a highly irrational use of geographical information.

Perhaps at this point in my argument my reader will be disposed to say to me, "You began by admitting that there was an Irish difficulty; you have since been occupied in proving (or attempting to prove) that the difficulty was not due to certain causes often alleged in explanation of it. But of what importance is this if the difficulty exists? You cannot cure a disease merely by exposing an incorrect diagnosis. So far you have not even suggested a diagnosis of your own."

The nature of the disease I have indicated. It is a sentiment of hostile and exclusive local patriotism, which deems itself outraged by the full inclusion of the locality on any terms, even the most generous, within a larger national unit. But if this be its nature, what is its explanation if we exclude as irrelevant or negligible differences of race, of institutions, of culture, or of geographical position?

The explanation is to be found in the tragic

coincidences of Irish history. The circumstances attending the slow increase of British power were in themselves a great misfortune. If Ireland had remained isolated from her neighbours she might gradually have evolved central institutions and a civilised polity of her own. If her warring clans had been rapidly and effectually subdued, as the Highland clans were subdued after the '45, the native Irish population might have immediately shared the advantages of the more advanced social and economic polity with which she had become associated.

But nothing could have been worse both for the English and the Irish than what actually occurred. Long continued guerrilla warfare is the most demoralising of all forms of warfare; and it never took a more demoralising form than it did in Ireland. To the English it was of slow and dubious advantage; to the Irish it was sheer loss. Yet the melancholy story would long ago have been forgotten and forgiven but for sectarian differences and agrarian wrongs. Unhappily it was impossible anywhere, in the sixteenth and seventeenth centuries, to exclude religion from politics; and it was certainly impossible in Ireland.

Do not, however, let us suppose that either the Protestants or the Roman Catholics concerned were of a type peculiarly bigoted or vindictive. As far as my knowledge goes this was not so. But unfortunately Ireland was dragged by British statesmen into the English and Scottish civil wars: in these religion and politics were inextricably mingled;

and the final defeat of James the Second left the majority of Irishmen convinced that the cause of Ireland was the cause of Roman Catholicism, and the majority of Englishmen convinced that the cause of Protestantism was the cause of Liberty. Ireland was divided into two camps; and divided into two camps she still remains.

What wars and massacres, confiscation and re-confiscation could not have done, has been effected by the combination of these with religious oppression. And though the days I am speaking of are long gone by, they have left behind them a tradition still sufficient to confer on Irish patriotism of the Nationalist type an anti-British flavour.

What, in these circumstances, should British statesmen do? In my personal opinion—I speak for no one but myself—there are only two policies open to them. They may maintain the Union and keep Ireland in full political communion with England and Scotland. Or they may give Ireland (with or without Ulster), complete autonomy, requiring her to manage her own finances, pay her own bills, borrow on her own credit, control her own rebels, settle her own constitution;—remaining, if she so desire it, a self-governing colony within the limits of the Empire.

This is evidently a counsel of despair. None of the great Dominions—not Canada, nor Australia, nor South Africa—would tolerate such a severance of their territories as is implied in this scheme. The United States has fought the bloodiest war of modern times in order to avoid it.

Yet the remedy, however desperate, is apparently suited to the disease. It gives Nationalist Ireland what it professes to desire: it should satisfy Irish patriotism in its narrowest and most hostile form. And those who really think that Ireland is a nation unrighteously held in bondage, or who deem that whether this be true or not, the majority of Irishmen will always think so, are bound to consider it. It is at least a solution of the Irish Nationalist problem; and this is more than can be said for Home Rule in any of its various shapes.

But if this complete surrender be regarded as impossible, can the alternative policy be persevered with? Can we remain as we are, refusing any concession to the hostile form of Irish patriotism whose origin I have endeavoured briefly to explain, and even in a measure to excuse?

I think we can; and I think so (in part) because neither reason nor experience suggests that this sentiment is destined to be eternal. Even now signs are not wanting that it is undergoing the same kind of change which has (for example) converted loyalty to the Stuart dynasty from a practical creed to an historic emotion. And the reasons are analogous. The wars and confiscations of the sixteenth and seventeenth centuries, the religious and economic injustices of the eighteenth, are long passed away; and there is no reason known to me why they should disturb the unity of the United Kingdom more permanently than the internecine horrors of the Thirty Years' War disturb the unity of a United Germany. If indeed Nationalists were expected by Unionists to sell their birthright, if the larger patriotism of a citizen of the Three Kingdoms was, in its essential nature, incompatible with the affection separately owed to each one by its children, we might well despair. But as I have tried to show, this is not the case. And even now those who will take the trouble to inquire may easily convince themselves how much there is of genuine Irish Nationalism which has no real desire either for independence or for Home Rule.

"But," it will perhaps be here objected, "you have so far not argued the case of Home Rule at all. You have discussed autonomy and (potential) separation; you have discussed the maintenance of the Union. The middle policy of Home Rule you have not discussed at all."

This is true. And the reason is that if the Irish difficulty is due to Irish Nationalism, Home Rule does not deserve to be described as a policy at all. It provides no solution of any Irish problem, or British problem either. It is not a constitutional remedy; it is a parliamentary device.

A very few words will make this clear. If the subject be approached from the side of the Irish nationality, which is the line of approach suggested by history and followed in this paper, the absurdities of Home Rule lie on the surface of the measure. The limitations imposed on the new Irish Parliament are such as were never desired by England in the case of the American Colonies before the War of Independence; nor would they ever

be tolerated by any one of the self-governing Dominions. How then can they be permanently accepted
by those whose policy is professedly based on the
indefeasible claims of Irish Nationality? And if
it be replied that the Nationalist members profess
themselves content, we are compelled to ask by what
right they attempt thus to set limits to the aspirations, in their opinion the just aspirations, of their
fellow-countrymen, either now or hereafter?

If again the subject be approached from the side
of constitutional equity or administrative convenience, the Bill is utterly without defence. No doubt
there are many persons who think that a large dele-
gation of parliamentary power to subordinate
assemblies would be a great constitutional reform.
I am not disposed to agree with them; but the case
is arguable. What is not arguable is the supposi-
tion that the Home Rule Bill is a serious contribution to this object. There is not in it from
beginning to end the faintest indication that its
authors ever supposed that its provisions could be
applied to other parts of the United Kingdom; nor
could they ever be so applied. In the meanwhile it
leaves Ireland grossly over-represented in the Imperial Parliament so far as English and Scottish
affairs are concerned, and grossly under-represented
so far as Imperial affairs are concerned. It gives
the Irish much more power than they ought to
have in moulding legislation which applies only to
Great Britain, and much less power than they ought
to have in controlling national policy and national
taxation. How can such a system last in Ireland?

How can it be extended to England or Scotland? How can it be seriously regarded as the solution of any problem whatever—national, constitutional, or administrative?

But if it solves no problem, it raises many, and of these the most urgent is Ulster. To the ordinary Radical voter in England or Scotland the evils of Home Rule may appear shadowy and remote. He regards the Irish question as a nuisance of long standing, and, if his leaders assure him that their scheme is going to bring it to an end, he is prepared to submit and pay. Very different is the feeling in the north-east of Ireland. There the maintenance of the Union is not deemed a matter of convenience or of personal sentiment: it is a matter of life and death; and as such, it will most certainly be treated.

And have the men of Ulster no justification for such a view? If the Irish of the south and west have an inherent moral right to claim administrative separation from the United Kingdom, has not Ulster an equal right to claim administrative separation from the rest of Ireland? If the Nationalist demand be founded upon race, is not Ulster in this respect as different from the rest of Ireland as the rest of Ireland is from England? If the Irish Nationalists profess to approve a plan which, like the Home Rule Bill, limits their rights as citizens of the United Kingdom, why should the wider patriotism of Ulster consent to the sacrifice? The Roman Catholics of the south and west certainly would not have considered themselves secure if, under whatever paper safeguards, they were placed in the power of the Ulster Protestants. Why should the Ulster Protestants be content to be placed in the power of Leinster, Munster, and Connaught? And if it be said that such a view ignores the modern spirit of religious toleration, I would remind the reader of what I have already insisted upon, namely, the historic part which religious differences have so unhappily played in the creation of the Irish problem. If England, through her misfortune or her fault, has been responsible for making Nationalist Ireland what it is, not less has she been responsible for making Unionist Ulster what it is; and the idea that Britain can save herself all further trouble by a partial and half-hearted withdrawal from Ireland, retaining the duty of protecting minorities, but abandoning all power of doing so effectually, seems to me to be, from the point of view of expediency, amazingly short-sighted, and, from the point of view of ethics, profoundly immoral.

My conclusion, then, from the arguments which I have indicated rather than expressed in any developed form, may be summarised as follows: The Irish problem, now that all Irish grievances connected with land, religion, and finance have been removed, is essentially due to the exclusive and often hostile form which Irish patriotism outside Ulster has assumed.

This finds no justification either in differences of race or in the memories of native institutions destroyed by foreign usurpation.

It has its origin in the unhappy circumstances of Irish history, and especially in the inevitable fusion, both in fact and in the memory of the Roman Catholic Irish, of wrongs due to religious divisions with others that followed on the heels of rebellion and civil war.

The memory of these unhappy events was kept alive long after the events were over by the social irritation due to one of the worst systems of land tenure which has ever existed; and though this and all the other causes which have produced the Irish problem are now removed, their effects, as is inevitable, survive them.

Those who think, as I do, that these effects are diminishing, and are destined to disappear, look forward to a time when Irish patriotism will as easily combine with British patriotism as Scottish patriotism combines now. They ask only for time, and not much of that. Although more than eighty years have passed since Roman Catholic disabilities were removed, yet it is only about a quarter of a century since the problem presented by the congested districts in Ireland began to receive special treatment; it is only about fifteen years since local government on a popular basis was set up; it is only about ten years since the land system was remodelled under the Wyndham Acts; and only about five years since provision was made to meet the special wants of the Roman Catholics in respect of university education. Measured by the standard of a nation's life such figures are insignificant. Give these remedial measures a chance, and do not in the meanwhile meddle with the constitution of the United Kingdom for other than purely administrative reasons. To those who reject this policy, who think that Irish patriotism, in its exclusive and more or less hostile form, is destined to be eternal, I would respectfully say that they must seriously face the question of giving Ireland outside Ulster complete autonomy even though this involves potential separation. Such a policy, however ruinous to Ireland, and however perilous to Great Britain, would at least satisfy the most extreme claims of Irish nationality; and nothing else will.

For these claims, if they are genuine, can never be satisfied by the Home Rule Bill; and if that Bill were really to put an end to the Nationalist agitation, it would be conclusive proof that the agitation was factitious, and that the cause of Irish patriotism in its exclusive form was already lost.

But if Home Rule cannot really satisfy Nationalist aspirations, from every other point of view it stands condemned. Financially, administratively, and constitutionally, it is indefensible; and considered from these points of view few indeed are the Home Rulers who sincerely attempt to defend it.

## 3

### ON INTERNATIONAL CONTACTS

*Speech at the Victoria Working Men's Club, Kew Gardens, July 24th, 1920*

I ENTERED Parliament many years ago—forty-six or forty-seven years ago—since which time I have been continuously engaged in the public service in one shape or another, under our singular but admirable British system—sometimes in the Government and sometimes in opposition, but always deeming, whether I was in the Government or in opposition, that I was doing my country a service. I don't know whether that view is commonly accepted —I think that we differ about it. Still, broadly speaking, so near are we in this country together, in the substantial basis of our opinions and the solid rock on which our convictions are based, that in truth the Government and the Opposition to-day have the same general ideas of public service, and it is recognised by their fellow-countrymen that they carry out, generally speaking, one broad ideal of public service. I think that is a most valuable peculiarity. It is rather a peculiarity of the British Constitution.

That invention of the King's Government and the King's Opposition, and what corresponds to it in other countries, I believe to be the essence of British freedom and of the working of constitutional liberty as we understand it. Why is it that that is a success?

I am not going to discuss questions in controversy between the parties, but there is nothing to prevent me from saying something regarding which all parties are agreed. If you get depressed as you may easily do at the signs of restlessness even in our own country, you will do well to remember that all sections of political life have a certain basis of political opinion, moderate in its character, reasonable in its execution, and never proceeding to extremes, making us—I think I may say this without national vanity—not necessarily the cleverest people in Europe, but the most reasonable people to deal with.

When I study foreign politics and note the extraordinary difficulties that beset foreign politicians in dealing with the problems presented to them by the public opinion of their own countries I feel that, however great our own difficulties, the task with which they have to deal is incomparably more perplexing, and incomparably more difficult of solution, and throws an incomparably heavier burden on those responsible for the conduct of public affairs.

There never was a time when the various peoples of the world were brought into closer contact with each other. All through the modern era the nations have been getting closer together from the point of view of trade, of manufactures and of industry.

Steadily a certain kind of intercourse has been made easier and easier by the facilities provided by railways, steamers and I suppose I ought to add, by aeroplanes.

But after all, these things do not bring you into close touch with the temperament, the psychology, the passions, the ambitions of your neighbours in other lands. It is another matter altogether to be brought, as we have been of recent years, into direct contact, sometimes into direct conflict, with nations of a different upbringing, a different history, a different psychology from ourselves. That is a new development forced not merely upon the statesmen, but the peoples of the various countries of Europe. Whether we like it or not, we are brought into immediate contact with each other. That is the destiny to which we are forced by circumstances. Like the members of the same family, we have got to live together. The members of a family may live together in peace and amity, mutual understanding and mutual good will, or they may quarrel, they may render life intolerable by their bickerings, they may render intercourse a source of endless pain and perplexity, instead of it being, as it ought to be, one of the greatest sources of mutual pleasure and satisfaction.

There are those who think that we in this country, because we are insular by geographical position, insular by political development, insular by individual growth in literature, art and religion, are less capable than others of comprehending those with whom we have to live in close international relationship.

I am not sure that that is so.  I admit the insularity; I admit too, that insularity carries with it some difficulties, some dangers; but I venture to say that it has produced in our people a spirit of moderation, and a power of mutual comprehension, which is the essential basis of all good human relationship.  I am not at all sure that this institution itself, the club which I am addressing, is not on a small scale an admirable example of those excellent qualities. What is the great advantage of a club of this sort? I have come across clubs more or less on similar lines.  There are clubs of different types, but all excellent, in the great working-class constituency which I represented for over twenty years in Lancashire.  I saw a great deal of them.  I believe that they do an admirable work.  They not only afford resources which the members do not obtain, and cannot obtain in the same measure, in their own homes, but they bring together people of different opinions upon all the great questions that more or less divide us, and make them feel that those who differ in opinion may yet have fundamental sympathies and agreements not to be expressed in political or social formulæ, but which lie at the very root of all sound human society.

After all, the world must depend on mutual charity, and mutual charity must depend upon mutual comprehension, and therefore I say that what we desire in international relations, the policy that we desire to see carried out, must, if it is to be successful, depend in the long run upon the nations learning to understand each other; and I would point this club as showing that outside international relations, on a small scale and in a comparatively narrow community, a club of this sort may carry out functions that we try, with more or less success, to carry out by international conferences and the League of Nations.

# 4
## On Nationality

*Opinions expressed in the course of a discussion on the Problem of Nationality at Oxford, September 28th, 1920*

A CERTAIN amount of criticism has been directed against the undue prominence which it is alleged has been given to the idea of nationality in reconstituting the map of Europe and bringing about the terms of peace. It is certainly possible to talk about the principle of nationality in language of absurd exaggeration, as if it were an eternal and immutable principle which has always governed, and ought always to govern, the constitution of human society, and as if the only problem that lies before the statesmen of the various countries is to see that this abstract and immutable principle shall be carried out without exception, and without lapse, in the case of every community throughout the world.

I take what I think is the plain common-sense view, that nationality is one of the methods of which humanity avails itself in the gradual evolution of civilisation, in order to act in some corporate capacity. This is an absolutely necessary thing for humanity to do. We are not all separate individuals, but members of a society, and the difficulty lies in constituting the society. The clan system, the city system, the feudal system, and the various imperial systems, have prevailed in different parts of the world at different ages, with more or less advantage.

The principle of nationality in its present full sense, and to its present extent, is rather a late growth. I entirely agree that it cannot be applied without exception throughout the whole realm of nature as if it were a mathematical principle—not to be changed as civilisation changes, but to remain the eternal measure and method by which human society should be constituted.

It can, however, be said of nationality that it lends itself to modern developments. It lends itself, I think better than any other system, to all the complex interests of a very highly complex modern community. Of all forms of producing human co-operation it is the one best adapted to democratic developments. I am inclined to believe that a full democratic constitution is by far the best for a modern homogeneous society, and that the best way of getting a modern homogeneous society is through the consciousness of nationality which enables people to work easily and naturally together. The future of democracy, however, is perhaps most in danger in those communities within whose boundaries there remain elements which are not homogeneous, and which do not therefore lend themselves to democratic institutions in the only true, effective and useful sense of the word.

The frontiers of the States of Europe cannot, however, be made precisely to conform to the lines dictated by nationality, however we may define that complicated idea. There are islands of alien population. It is evident that these cannot be given a separate national existence. It is the duty of all these sections of population, who find themselves members of a nation which they regard as alien for linguistic, racial, religious or any other reasons, to subordinate their natural feeling of nationalism to the greater whole. Nationality is valuable, in so far as it is a centripetal principle, and in so far as it produces closer co-operation between members of a human race. It has another side, and it must not be put on an absurd pedestal. It is not to any politician's or stateman's credit to work on the emotions of nationality to produce division; the proper use of the feeling of nationality is to produce union.

## 5
## On the Party System in Politics

*Speech at the Annual Dinner of the United Wards Club of the City of London, December 15th, 1908*

I do not deny that there may be disadvantages— in fact, there are disadvantages—in the party system, but nobody has ever devised a better plan with which to deal with great assemblies, and inasmuch as nobody has ever invented any method of carrying on free government—by which I understand government as far as may be by public opinion—except through the medium of discussion in large assemblies, I do not see that we can avoid the party system, however great may be the evils incident to it. The objections, of course, are obvious, but the objections to any other system would, I am convinced, in practice be found still more obvious; and if you are going to break up the dual party system which now exists in this country into a series of groups, each coagulating round a particular leader, combining, perhaps, to form a Government, and then to destroy the Government, and to form a new Government, and then to destroy that Government, you will, I believe, bring Parliamentary institutions into profound discredit, and you will render impossible that continuity of adminis-

tration which, even in the hands of those from whom
I profoundly dissent, I believe to be the only possible
way of carrying on the government of this country.

I would much rather have in power a Radical
Government—and everybody here knows I dissent
from Radical Governments—carrying on the administration of the country, with some security that
they have behind them the support of an organised
party, than see the administration of a complicated
Empire like our own bandied about from side to
side, from group to group, from small section to
small section, preyed upon first by this political adventurer and then by that political adventurer—a
method by which the whole system would be brought
into hopeless disrepute.  If you are to have the party
system at all—and I think you must have it—I do
not think it has worked in any country in the world
so well as it has worked in our country.

Foreigners, whenever they come to our shores,
are amazed that men of different political complex-
ions, belonging to different and rival parties, should
be able to meet, not merely in a friendly spirit
socially, but to carry on, or assist each other, in
those great departments of public work in which
politics do not come in.  We are able to do that
in this country.  No doubt anybody who is prepared to ransack with a malignant eye the history
of this country for the last two hundred years will
find cases, perhaps many cases, in whch party
spirit really has done some deep injury to the interests, the external policy, of the country; but I
do not believe there ever was a country, ruled in

that fashion and by those forces, which has found itself so able as we have found ourselves to surmount the inevitable dangers and weaknesses of the party system, and, where great national needs required it, to sink domestic differences in the face of dangers which threatened the community as a whole.

I do not believe that the present House of Commons is in these respects worse than its predecessors. It is a curious fact that general opinion —which, after all, is the responsible author and creator of the House of Commons—is always abusing it. You are responsible for it, gentlemen. It is the electors of this country who have brought it into being, and it is not for them really to attack its constitution. The individuals who differ from its existing constitution have, no doubt, thrown upon them the incumbent duty of changing its party complexion at the first opportunity, but the general character of the individuals, apart from their politics, the class of men who are returned, rests with the electors of this country, and it is not for them to abuse the general character of the assembly. It is for them to change it if they dislike it.

I am not in the least a pessimist about the future of this country. I do not believe that you are going to abolish the House of Lords. I do not believe that you are going to destroy the House of Commons. Those two assemblies have now for centuries—with mistakes, of course, many mistakes, countless mistakes—carried on the continuous tradition of the liberty of this country, and I do not believe that you are likely to improve upon the machinery—the broader aspects of it—by which such great results have been achieved in the past, and by which, as I think, equal results are to be attained in the future.

At this moment I am convinced that if you want really to learn the arguments pro and con upon any controverted question of politics, you will find it better in the debates of the House of Commons and the House of Lords than you will find it in any Blue Books, leading articles, monthly reviews, or any other source to which you can turn. Of course, there are dull speeches delivered, stupid speeches, boring speeches, irrelevant obstructionist speeches that miss the point, that are merely occupied with the claptrap of the platform. All that is quite true of the House of Commons. The House of Lords may have its defects, but it rises above those particular weaknesses.

Although that may be true of the House of Commons, it still is true that a really good debate in the House of Commons puts from side to side the main outlines of a controversy in a way in which you will not find it done anywhere else, and I do not agree with those who think that our debates are contemptible. They may be dull, they certainly are rarely eloquent, but I believe that matters in dispute are dealt with with great acumen, often with great knowledge, and that we are not unworthy of the great confidence which the country places in us.

# 6

## ON THE HOUSE OF COMMONS

*Speech at the Banquet given by the Lord Mayor of London to the Masters of the Livery Guilds, March 11th, 1909*

THERE are some matters connected with the two great bodies with which we are dealing, the Houses of Lords and Commons, which I hope are not destined to change or alter with the changings and alterings of passions of the moment, but which are predestined through generations still to come to serve the future as they have served the past, to minister to the needs of the great community which owes so much of its greatness, so much of its freedom, and so much of its prosperity to the joint effort of Lords and Commons.

With regard to the House of Lords, I am surely not going beyond what every impartial observer will admit when I say that, at all events, of many of the great Imperial subjects which are and which ought to be our main preoccupation, the debates of the House of Lords are, to put it mildly, as instructive as the debates in the House of Commons.

Is it not of immense advantage to a country like our own, which has interests so diverse and so far-reaching, that there shall be a body like the House of Lords, full of men of experience in different spheres of responsibility, not dependent upon this or that chance vote, or the strength of some temporary current which is set in motion, perhaps, by some passing and soon-forgotten influence; that there should be a Chamber where men of mature years and wide experience should find an audience, and themselves have an opportunity of speaking with authority on matters so close to the deepest interests of the community? I cannot forbear pointing out these merits in the composition of the House of Lords.

As for the composition of the House of Commons, nobody ever tries to question that. They regard it for good or for evil as part of the order of nature to which we must submit, whether we like it or not. All Houses of Commons in my experience, however much I may differ individually from the opinions of the majority, have, I think, shown a great faculty for parliamentary government, which is a hereditary possession of our race.

Of course, I do not claim for our House that everybody in it is able, is virtuous, is eloquent, or unprejudiced. I make no such preposterous claims for a great political assembly. Indeed, I do not see how the government of the country could be carried on at all if, instead of being six hundred gentlemen of, I hope, average character and ability, we were six hundred gentlemen all inspired with the eloquence of Demosthenes and Cicero. It is quite certain we should not do business, and I never join myself with those who regret that there are not a

very much larger number of men whose eloquence
rivals that of the Pitts, the Chathams, and the Foxes.
But whether we do good or bad, do not let the outside British public criticise us too severely, and for
this reason—it is the outside British public that
made us: they are responsible for us. If we hold
wrong opinions, it is the public who are responsible.
It is no use saying, "There is the House of Commons doing this foolish thing and that foolish
thing, wasting its time in that way or in this way,"
for you are the authors of our corporate being, and
you have no right to abuse our handiwork. If that
handiwork can be improved, the proper way to do it
is not to abuse the representatives you have sent to
the House. If you think they are wrong, send different people there.

Remember that it is folly to criticise a representative assembly. The whole responsibility rests with
the electors. We do our best. We have been sent
there as representing certain schools of opinion.
We work very hard, and if the policy that we promote is not the policy by which the real interests of
the Empire can be promoted, if the principles which
animate us are not those which wise statesmanship
and far-seeing policy recommend, it is the public—
and the public alone—who are responsible for that
state of things, and the public—and the public alone
—who can remedy it.

## 7

### On the House of Lords

*Speech at the Dinner of the City of London Conservative Association, March 4th, 1910*

WHAT justification can there be for those who, like myself, think there ought to be some change in the constitution of the Second Chamber? I will tell you what my view is on that point. It is not that the House of Lords, as at present constituted, is not efficient. It is efficient. Never have its debates been at a higher level. Never has it held more men of great experience, of great knowledge of affairs, and great public spirit. Never has it shown itself, in my opinion, more capable of doing that which it is one of the main businesses of a Second Chamber to do—namely, to see that any great and fundamental change in our Constitution or in our practice should be submitted to the considered judgment of the country. It is not that the House of Lords lacks efficiency: it is that, in the present condition of public opinion, it lacks strength—it lacks that kind of strength which would enable it to defy the sort of attack which has been most absurdly, as I think, and scandalously made upon it during the course of our recent political controversies.

Now, I do not want a better Second Chamber.

I want a stronger Second Chamber. I know no source from which that additional strength can be obtained, than that from which the House of Commons derives all its power—namely, the feeling that there is some direct and formal connection between public opinion and the Second Chamber. But I do hope we shall all remember certain broad principles which ought to govern, as I think, every man who attempts to touch the immemorial Constitution of this country.

In the first place let us remember that we do not want in a Second Chamber a copy of the First Chamber. We do not want a Second Chamber to be another House of Commons. That would be to deprive the Second Chamber of all its value as a wheel in the constitutional machine, as a part of the system by which progress is made steady, cautious, permanently effective. What you want in the Second Chamber is not a repetition or a rival of the First Chamber. What you want is a Chamber which shall not arrogate to itself, as foreign Second Chambers too often have done, powers of the immediately representative Chamber, which gradually suck from that Chamber all its authority and power and which make the directly representative Chamber play but a second rôle in the Constitution of the country.

I, being a member of the House of Commons, should look with great dismay upon a change in the fate of the House of Commons comparable to that which has befallen either the representative Assembly in France or the representative Assembly in the

United States of America. That, I think, is the principle to remember.

The second principle is that if you were to carry that out you must have men who are not immediately amenable, as we in the House of Commons cannot help being, to two influences. The one is the passing passion of the moment; the other is the electoral machine, the caucus, or whatever you choose to call it. In the House of Commons it is extremely difficult for the independent thinker—at all events the independent speaker—to subsist, still less to flourish. He finds great difficulty when the moment comes round for his election. I do not want in either Assembly too many crotcheteers, too many doctrinaires, too many men who preach their own particular fancy and refuse to work with the great bodies of their fellow-countrymen; but it would be surely a great misforune if it were impossible in either Chamber to find a place for those men who by temperament, by tradition, or by training could not fit themselves into the party system, and who, because they cannot fit themselves into the party system, find it hard to obtain, or if they obtain it, find it hard to retain, a place in the House of Commons. They can find a place, and do find a place, in the House of Lords, and whenever they find it they retain it.

Above all, we want in the Second Chamber a Chamber which, although not too powerful, is powerful enough to resist the temporary gust of the moment, and which represents more accurately, perhaps than the House of Commons can ever represent, not the passing mood of the people, but the permanent wishes of the nation. One other general maxim I would venture to lay down is this. If there be any lesson to be learned from historic tradition it is that in England at least, no revolution is permanent which does not take account of the past. Whatever our Second Chamber is to be in the future, let it be the natural development under modern conditions of that great constitutional and historic past which has made us what we are.

Innovation may be necessary—for my own part I think it is necessary—but let it be an innovation deeply based upon the history of our country, impregnated in every part with the memory of what has been before, for it is only if we follow out that tradition that you will be able to make those reforms which, in their turn, last and form a stage in the development of the nation, and on those conditions alone your reform will be of a kind on which our children and grandchildren, looking back, will say: England has ever been a country where institutions have grown, not a country where institutions are cut down and new ones planted.

# 8

## On the House of Lords

*Speech at the Dinner of the City Lands Committee of the Corporation, April 16th, 1913*

I DO not know whether we ought to attach any great value to foreign criticism. Outsiders, they say, see most of the game, and that is true. Yet it is difficult for a foreigner to judge of anything so characteristically insular as British politics, and certainly I should not desire to attach any excessive value to opinions which, though quite impartial, though formed entirely outside our domestic controversies and quarrels, are yet necessarily formed with imperfect knowledge of the facts. But it is a disquieting reflection to know that, so far as my experience goes, foreigners who give their minds to these constitutional questions, who desire, as we all desire whatever our politics may be, that we should be governed by two Chambers—two Chambers above all suspicion, from every point of view, of character and capacity, carrying them with the assent and the admiration of the democracy which has called them into being—those foreigners who share with us those ideals, and desire to see British traditions of constitutional liberty more and more carried into happy fruition in other great communities, look with the deepest disquiet upon the trend of public events during the last half generation.

I do not know whether they are right. I myself have always been an optimist about the House of Commons. I have been a member of that assembly with but one brief break of a few days, since 1874. I have been interested in its traditions and in its history, and I am not prepared to admit that all the criticisms that I hear about our deterioration of manners and the inferiority of our speaking are true. But I have to admit that I think we stand less well in the opinion of the country. I do not think that a debate in the House of Commons is looked to in all parts of the Kingdom and abroad, and among our fellow-subjects across the seas, with the same respect or interest or attention as it was when I was a younger politician.

If that be so it is a great tragedy. It is a tragedy which has its parallels—indeed which is exceeded in other countries. Those who are, as I am, sincerely democratic, in the sense of saying that the deliberate will of the community must prevail —those who share those views with me must, I think, be alarmed at the fact that in so many countries where democracy, so far as paper Constitutions can make it, really rules the whole destinies of the nation, democracy seems incapable in many cases of creating an Assembly representing itself, to which it can pay the smallest possible tribute of respect.

We have not got to that. Let us reflect whether we are not getting towards it. If I am right, it

is the most serious danger ahead of free institutions
throughout the world, and in my gloomier moments
I often think that perhaps the optimism in which,
basing myself purely on British history, I still in-
dulge, may not in the long run, and after my public
career is over, show itself in a steady deterioration
of the credit in which the House of Commons stands
—and perhaps not merely the House of Commons,
but that future Second Chamber, which in some
shape or another is quite certain to have elective
element in it.   May I on that subject observe that,
speaking as a member of the House of Commons,
I see not merely the general tendency of which I
have spoken common to all free Constitutions, I see
not merely that danger ahead of us, I see other
dangers peculiar to ourselves.

The course of the recent constitutional changes
has been, as we all know, to limit—as some people
think to destroy—the power of the Second Chamber to do the work of a Second Chamber.  It is also
true that both parties are agreed that when the
Second Chamber is remodelled it must include a
large representative element.

I am not going to discuss alternative schemes
of reform of the Second Chamber, but I am going
to say that I am quite certain that in proportion as
you make the Second Chamber a representative
chamber, in that proportion you give the power now
held by the House of Commons to the Second Chamber.  The second Chamber in our Constitution, an
hereditary Second Chamber, has never been able, or
at all events has not been able for much more than

a century, even to embarrass a Government, except in debate, and except, it may be, as regards the details of Bills. It has never been able to threaten their existence. Do you suppose that a Second Chamber, if it became an elective Chamber, is not going to follow the example set us by the Senate of the United States and the Senate of the French Chamber? Do you suppose that a Second Chamber, when it has behind it an electorate, is not going to say, "We represent that electorate just as much as the House of Commons?" Of course it is. And therefore, I, as a member of the House of Commons, devoted to that assembly in which I have spent all the working years of my life, say that, whether it be good on the whole for the community, whether Parliament is going to be a greater Parliament in the future than it has been in the past, at all events, when all these changes and reforms are carried out, it is going to be a different Parliament. In that Parliament, if you take all the influences at work against the credit of the House of Commons, often wrongly, in my opinion, but sometimes rightly— and you have a Second Chamber with the authority which the class of men elected to the Second Chamber carry with them in other countries, and with the consciousness that they not less than the House of Commons represent the general public opinion—do not tell me that the glories of the House of Commons will not suffer some eclipse. It will no longer be the Chamber to which, ever since the days of Sir Robert Walpole, a man who desired really to influence his countrymen, really to be an effective leader of the political life of those around him, has wished to belong.

You will alter the whole centre of gravity of politics. A man will say, "Well, if I desire to take part in the politics of my country I would rather be a member of the Second Chamber, I should carry more weight in the Second Chamber; I should be a more important man in the Second Chamber than if I belong to the Chamber which at present immediately represents the people of this country."

I do not see that there is any possibility of avoiding that development on the lines on which we are now going. And, though it will all happen after my time, I frankly admit that I, who love the House of Commons, who look at its history with pride and affection, should be deeply grieved to see that the undisputed weight which it has hitherto held for a century and a half in dealing with the affairs of this great free community should be in large part handed over to a Second Chamber which, however constituted, would neither be the old House of Commons nor the old House of Lords.

# 9

## ON SOCIALISM

*Speech at a Unionist Demonstration in Peebles, October 23rd, 1924*

YOUR Chairman has told you what is surely the truth, that this election is unique in its character, unique in the issues which it involves.

All of us here, even the youngest of us, have seen more than one election.  I, who am far from being the youngest among you, have seen a great many in the course of what is now a very long political life.  But never, either in my time or in the time of our fathers before us, has an issue comparable to the one with which we now have to deal been brought before the electors for their decision.

I do not think that that issue is thoroughly realised.  We are all habituated in this happy island of ours to a continuity of policies, to a system which progressed unhurt and uninterrupted gradually from generation to generation, solidifying and strengthening the liberties of the country, with our prosperity growing, our population increasing, our Empire stretching over every quarter of the globe.  Our history, with all its changes, is absolutely continuous in character; and we have a well-founded reputation in every country in the world for the manner in which we have continued to harmonise progress with stability, the readiness to lead the very van of civilisation, and yet to feel that we have behind us a vast tradition, and that in modifying its organism to meet new conditions, we are but carrying on the traditions of our remotest forefathers.

Does anybody suppose that if this election were to put a Socialist Government in fully responsible office, that that continuity which I have ventured to describe in no exaggerated terms would any longer be the boast of our country and our race? What is the question? The great question is whether you will tear up by the roots the whole moral and economic policy upon which civilisation has hitherto been founded, on which, as I believe, the future of civilisation absolutely depends, and which, in all our controversies in the past, in all the battles between Whig and Troy, or between Liberal and Unionist in days more modern, was left untouched. Socialists would not deny that they propose a complete revolution in the economic and the juridical policy of the country. They would not deny it. They would boast of it. They would say, "That is why we are Socialists, that is what we want to do." Perhaps they would go on and say, "After all this is a conflict between the 'haves' and the 'have nots,' between the rich and poor, between those who have been fortunate in their lot in life and those who have been unfortunate."

That is a profoundly misleading account of the real issue. It is very easy to make the rich poor. All efforts of mankind, all the inventions of men of science, and of natural philosophy, all the progress of education, has done much, and may do much more, to better the lot of the great mass of humanity. But do not for one minute believe that the difficulty lies in a conflict between rich and poor. The real point is this—Under what industrial system do we get the best results for the well-being of the great mass of the people?

The system which now prevails does produce a certain number of rich men. The question still remains—Would any system you may propose to substitute diminish the number of poor men? It is perfectly easy to equalise down; the problem of the statesman is to do what he can to equalise up.

It is a simple task, or would be a simple task, for some absolute ruler to reduce all his subjects to a lot little better than that of the beast, but it requires much more than power, it requires knowledge, wisdom, scientific perception of facts to raise any population above the level. There the statesman or philanthropist finds himself. That is the part which lies before us, and, believe me, that part can never be accomplished if you approach it in the spirit of those who think that by merely confiscating capital, and appropriating wealth for the State, they are moving a step towards giving us the social machinery we require.

That is the profoundest of all mistakes. It assumes that there is international wealth as a fixed quantity which you can cut up and divide at the will of the legislature. National wealth is due to a daily process. Day by day it is being made, day by day it is being used, and our task is to preserve what we inherit of the machinery for producing this wealth, and to better it if we can.

May I venture to illustrate these general remarks by some more complete observation with regard to the particular position of this country. We live, every one of us, in this tightly packed island of ours, the most closely packed population in the world, the most absolutely dependent upon itself, not merely upon its internal trade but upon its foreign trade.

Many nations there are who depend for their luxuries upon what they can import from abroad, but who, as regards the essentials of life, are wholly self-supporting. We are not in that happy category. It is absolutely necessary for this island to sell abroad. If we do not sell abroad we cannot purchase from abroad. It is not merely that we lose our wealth. It is not merely that our prosperity vanishes like a cloud, it is that we cease to exist, or to put it more shortly, it is that we starve. On that point I imagine that we all take the same view. None so ignorant as not to know that, whatever you do for agriculture, or whatever agriculture does for itself, our population will still require foreign food merely to keep body and soul together.

To get foreign food we must induce foreign countries to purchase our goods. We must produce these goods so efficiently that the world is willing to purchase them, and to purchase them in sufficient quantities. We cannot sell unless we are efficient, and unless we sell we starve, and observe that our position is one far less secure than it was in the time of our fathers. In the times of our fathers and grandfathers Great Britain had a manufacturing monopoly. It led the world. It had a natural position of superiority which made foreign competition of no very serious moment in the national economy.

These happy days of security are gone by. Other nations have known how to follow where we led the way. Other nations have shown that they can use our methods—in some respects, I fear, they improve upon our methods—and therefore in our competition with the world we run greater risks, we look for greater difficulties than those which beset our happier predecessors.

Does anybody think, does any Socialist think, that our position in the markets of the world is so secure that we can afford to adopt methods and to practise devices which no other nation practises, no other nation uses, and which surely every man of sense must see will in the long run be fatal to our productive proficiency? Remember that Great Britain is a vast organised hive of industry, but that the machinery of that industry is a delicate machinery.

It might have been supposed that under a Socialist regime a country like Russia, with its vast population, its illimitable resources, its boundless expanse of food-bearing country, might play any tricks it liked with its economic system. As a matter of fact we know that that is not so, and that even Russia is sinking by reason of its neglect, its contemptuous destruction of all the economic machinery of civilisation.

Now I should like to ask anybody who criticises
these statements, where they see a weak point in the
argument? Let me just in two or three words repeat it. We live by inducing other populations over
whom we have not control, to take our goods. We
can only induce them to take our goods if we produce these goods as efficiently, as cheaply or more
cheaply, than those of our rivals, and we cannot do
that under modern conditions unless we reach the
highest point of industrial efficiency. The whole
teaching of modern Socialism appears to me to forget that elementary fact. They do not consider output. At any rate they do not consider it with a
view to increasing it. Output and production of
wealth is that on which we live, quite irrespective
of how it is distributed.

I was very much amused at some observations
which Mr. Ramsay MacDonald made in one of his
speeches. He said: "How the Tories and the
Liberals ought to thank God for Russian Bolsheviks!
There is no bogy like it, and how can they live without bogies? A bogy is essential to the interests of
reaction in the country."

I quite agree that if by a bogy you mean an object-
lesson, Bolshevist Russia is an object-lesson. I also
agree that Unionists and Liberals point to this
object-lesson often and effectively; but the reason
they always point to Bolshevist Russia as an evidence of the failure of Socialistic and Communistic
theories, is that there is no other country which has
had the folly to adopt those methods. It is the one
country where you can show such theories carried

to their logical conclusion in a great nation, carried out by the Government of a great nation. I suppose experience is something that we ought occasionally to appeal to. If an experiment has been tried on a great scale and has failed, if that experiment has been tried on a great scale nowhere else, because it is believed in nowhere else, it surely does not show a perverse mind, or a dulled intellect, to point to the examples, whether they be called examples of a bogy or not.

But really the calm confidence with which Socialists talk Socialism in the face of this, and of those lesser experiments which have been tried in the course of the last hundred years, fills me with astonishment. There have been Socialist communities consisting of picked enthusiasts. You cannot have a whole community consisting of picked enthusiasts—and that may be a reason for only trying the Socialist experiment on a small scale when you can get exactly the people with the right qualifications for carrying it out, but even with all those advantages, every one of the elaborate experiments has been a colossal tragedy. It has never succeeded; it has most usually failed ludicrously.  *54101*

Then comes along the one great case on the other side, the one great case of a whole nation of one hundred million, or a hundred and twenty million, driven, whether they like it or not, to try this experiment. That experiment from no point of view whatever has succeeded; from the logical point of view it has utterly failed, because the Bolshevist Government began by announcing that all property of every kind—land, capital, machinery and the rest of it—belong to the State. But the Russian peasants, who happen to be a very large majority of the population, calmly ignore this statement of principle, and to this day remain owners of their holdings, just as if no Bolshevist Government had been in existence. I do not say that their lot is not deeply affected by what Bolshevism has done for them. Means of communication have utterly failed, and therefore when the periodical famines visit a particular district it is impossible, even if the Government were prepared, to bring from other parts of Russia food which Russia could undoubtedly supply, had the ordinary civilised machinery of government been kept in order by the present holders of power in Russia. It has equally failed from every point of view with regard to the town worker. His position is miserable; there is no question of freedom, there is no question of strikes, there is no question of anything but sullen obedience.

In effect that Government have destroyed capital, they have destroyed credit, they have destroyed all the three requisites of efficient production, and they have done that in the interest of the worker, whom they have ruined; the agriculturist, whom they have suppressed. They are not content with that. Having destroyed all capital, having destroyed all credit at home, they then turned to what they called the bourgeois Government of Great Britain, and they say: "There ought to be no capital, you are a capitalist country, your very existence is an offence, but as you happen to have capital, although there ought to be none, we should like to have forty or fifty millions from you to set us on our economic legs again." Now that is Mr. Ramsay MacDonald's bogy. If he can point to any community outside Russia where we can study the effects of his policy under favourable circumstances, there is not one of us that would not be glad to study it. Russia is not so agreeable a spectacle that I want to keep my eyes firmly fixed on it. I keep my eyes firmly fixed on Russia because there is no other Socialist country to look at.

Now I only want to say one more thing. If the account that I have given of Socialism in practice be true, and if the account that I have also given of the necessities of the British community be also true, you may well ask whether there is the slightest possibility that any body of successful Britishers, whatever their class, their training, habits or education, would ever tolerate such a change in our immemorial system.

I do not think that there is the smallest chance of this experiment being tried for any length of time. The whole population would rise in infuriated horror if we were suddenly to be offered all the rich blessings of Soviet rule. I am therefore not the least afraid that society in Great Britain is ever going to be organised on lines like these, but I am afraid that in some rash moment an experiment might be tried for a brief time. Believe me, even the briefest experiment spells ruin to a community like ours, so elaborate, so sensitive is the machinery of credit and of industry, so easy is it for prosperity to take wings and fly to countries more wisely and soberly governed. The very thought, if it were once entertained generally, of such expedients as capital levy, and the placing of vast tracts of industry into the grip of a bureaucracy at Whitehall, would cause an immediate disaster, a disaster which would fall on every mother, and every cottage in the country. I am at a loss to frame a picture of what would happen if we become unable to pay, as we should become under a Soviet regime, for our necessary imports and our necessary raw materials, the very things on which we live and prosper. That machinery, all-important, critical, delicate as it is, would be shattered by an experiment, even if six months after the experiment were begun, its authors in terror endeavoured to put an end to it.

You cannot play fast and loose with these ancient growths of civilisation. You must use them, you may improve them, you ought to improve them, but you cannot substitute a new social economy in a country like ours. The idea that you can do that is totally unworthy of the character and the ability of the people who are preaching it. If it is tried you can never withdraw from it, you can never reverse it without having undergone a national disaster impossible to calculate, impossible accurately to foresee, but which would exceed in magnitude, and in unhappy consequences, any calamity which so far has befallen our great and hitherto prosperous community.

## 10

## On Class War

*February 17th, 1925*

I AM a Conservative because I am absolutely certain that no community in this world has ever flourished or could ever flourish if it was faithless to its own past. What does Conservative mean? It means that the population of this country feels that it has inherited a great tradition, and means to use that tradition, not in any spirit of slavish conformity to ideas which in their particular form might be outworn, but because they are determined to build solidly for the future, and they know that unless they build solidly on the past their building will never stand the stress and storm by which every living community, every great historical nation, is from time to time threatened.

I like the name Unionist because the merits of union are too little remembered, and too little valued in these times, and because, if the British Empire is to be in the future the bulwark of liberty, freedom, and progress, which it has always been in the past, the members of that Empire, in spite of separating seas, must never forget their common origin, never allow their patriotism to grow cold, but must feel with ever-increasing strength, as the years go on, how very close ought to be the bond which unites all these free, self-governing unities into one coherent and civilising Empire.

I have talked of Imperial union; let me say a word about social union. No more abominable creed has ever been preached than that creed invented at the very climax of our so-called civilisation—the creed of class warfare. It is abominable, in my judgment, from every point of view. It is abominable from the moral point of view, and it is abominable from the material point of view. No prosperity, no success, no diminution in the social evils by which we are surrounded can ever be expected or will ever flow from a creed based upon hatred. It is not merely immoral, it is also extraordinarily stupid. After all, mankind lives upon the co-operative effort of its citizens for producing the necessaries of life and the well-being of life—all the elements which make for material and moral prosperity.

Co-operation was, and must be, at the base of every species of success, and it is an insane illusion to suppose that without co-operation we can obtain success and have all the fruits of peace. If such an idea were allowed to penetrate into the feelings and consciences of the mass of our population, it would undoubtedly spell the ruin of all classes. It has spelt ruin for every community where it has been tried, and there is no community in the world which can less afford to make those perilous experiments, and to absorb this social poison, than our own.

The future of this country ultimately depends on co-operation, friendliness, mutual good-will and service, and all classes working together for one great object.

That is a lesson too often forgotten in our political and municipal fights. Some there are, who are always urging on some pernicious quarrel, because it is a quarrel, who are always delighted to see a bitter controversy raging, because it is bitter. Such men, far from being alarmed or depressed at the prospect of a social ruin of which the working classes would be the greatest victims, rejoice in it, and say that they would like to start afresh to build up a society from the wreck they had left. How can we describe such leaders? How can they help anybody? To me their doctrines appear sheer insanity.

I have now in the natural course of events but a few years in which to see the results of the many forces which are now moulding and moving society, but I should look in despair at the future of my country if I thought that experiments like those were likely to be tried by these reckless professors of novelty.

In this vast metropolis there will be another great trial of strength not many days hence. Let nobody think that the municipal elections in London do not compare in importance with the political efforts which are perhaps of a more showy character.

Unless these people of ours, leaders in local self-government, born in it from their cradle, can manage the affairs of the great city which is in their keeping, they will show themselves unworthy of the great destiny which Providence has given them.

SECTION III
# THE MODERN STATE

I

## On Religious Education

*Speech at a Meeting of the National Society for Religious Education, June 2nd, 1913*

THE division between religious and secular training is fundamentally erroneous. It implies a dualism of object which I am convinced no thinking man, whatever his beliefs are, can really approve of. A secular psychologist might say he did not approve of religious training, but if he were a man who knew his business he would say: If religious training is a good thing, do not attempt to force it from the general training of the mind, do not put it into a separate compartment to be dealt with on entirely different principles and for entirely different objects.

The training of the children and young people of a country is, and must be, an organic whole. You cannot cut it up into separate compartments, and a school is not, and ought not to be, a place merely contrived to fill to the brim some unfortunate child, with what is called secular learning. The object of education is training, and training is an indivisible whole. I grant that towards this indivisible object both the home and the school must contribute.

If you could get an ideal home in which not

only the moral and religious characteristics of the parents were highly developed, but in which they had at their command all the necessary secular learning, in some senses a better training would be given than in any school, except in respect of the education a boy derives by mixing with other boys. But when you are dealing with a population of 36,000,-000 in England and Wales, and when you consider the conditions under which most of the parents work, it is quite impossible that, whatever their will and their moral qualifications, they could do all the work of training which is required. That is universally recognised. If it is admitted that you cannot bisect education into secular on the one side, and religious on the other, it follows inevitably that you ought to provide that kind of religious training, if any, which the parents desire, in the schools to which you compel them to send their children. That proposition follows with an irresistible logic from premises universally accepted. Why, then, is not this simple piece of logic embodied in actual legislation, and given practical effect in all the schools in the country?

The difficulties are practical rather than theoretical. It is very hard so to arrange matters while the State thinks it is out of its power to help this or that religious denomination. All that you can do is to mould your system, which has grown up under the pressure of very different forces, which has never been symmetrically arranged from the beginning, and is not now a symmetrical system logically defensible in every part. All you can do is to mould it gradually so as to ensure that religious education shall not be severed from secular education, and that the religious education shall be the religious education desired by the parents of the child.

If the whole system of voluntary teaching were to break down, who could doubt that a blow of the deadliest kind would have been levelled at the educational ideal of the great body of public opinion throughout the country, which firmly believes it is madness to bring up the rising generation without some belief in the worship of the Unseen? None could doubt the effect would be disastrous, and they would be left face to face with a system which was secular by essence, and religious only by accident, and which had not side by side with it the perpetual stimulus which the example of denominational schools gives to the undenominational schools.

If once that ideal got fixed in the public mind I believe the loss would be quite incalculable. I do not think any legislation could put that right. You would have lost something of the past which no efforts in the present or future could give back to you. Once done it could never be restored, and no public conviction, no remorseful, backward looks towards the past, no lamentations over the loss of great things which once we owned, would have the slightest effect, or help in the smallest degree to give you back that which your own carelessness has thrown away.

I do not deny there are great difficulties in carrying out the ideal of providing religious education in conformity with the wishes of the parent. Yet I think we are in some respects more hopefully situated for their solution than we were when I first entered public life.  I am convinced that those who lead the thought of the country are far less enamoured of the secular ideal than they were thirty years ago.  I notice the same feeling of uneasiness growing in other countries than our own over the loss that a community must suffer which permits itself to lapse into the slough of mere materialism, speculative or practical.  You will find thinkers not very well disposed towards Christianity, certainly with no special claims to orthodoxy, looking uneasily at the results which the secularisation of education is producing.

That is one hopeful sign.  Another is that, unless I misread the trend of contemporary thought, Christians of all denominations are turning their gaze more and more steadily upon those things they hold in common, without in the least becoming indifferent to those points which separated them one from the other.  I think they are seeing these things in a different perspective from what they did when I was a young man, and there is a keener desire among the leaders of the Churches to emphasise as far as possible those great verities upon which all Christians are agreed, and not to attach undue emphasis to those points on which differences still inevitably remain.

That is a most wholesome frame of mind, for one reason, among others, that it no longer takes the simple form of saying, "Well, if Christians differ, if one denomination holds Christianity in one shape, and another denomination holds it in another shape, the State has only to make some kind of distillation from these various creeds, get at what is common to all of them, put it in a separate vessel, and say that it is what every taxpayer may be asked to contribute to without injuring his conscience."

That is a preposterous doctrine. It may have been tolerable in the Middle Ages that there should be a forced contribution for an undivided Church which had, or conceived it had, Divine sanction and a history going back far beyond the history of any secular State, but the idea is absurd that in the twentieth century you are going to have a forcible levy in order to teach at the public expense something which a Department and the Law Courts between them might extract from an Act of Parliament, as being the common elements of Christianity.

I think that the Churches are beginning to see that, while it is quite possible to have excellent religious teaching in elementary schools, the force behind it all must be the organised force of Churches. It could not be the organised force of the ratepayers or of the Education Department, or of the County Council.

Therefore, the moral of it all is this—Encourage parents as far as you can to feel that religious education is absolutely necessary for their children. Exercise upon those parents no pressure as to what that religious education should be. They may happen to approve of the religious education given in some particular provided school in their neighbourhood, and excellent some of that teaching is. If, on the other hand, they prefer that the teaching should have behind it the authority of the Church to which they belong, then do not deprive the children of Churchmen of the privilege which they now possess, and for which they pay most dearly, in order to attain to some kind of symmetry which, if attained, would defeat its own ends. Use all the influence at your disposal and all your tact to induce those responsible for the education of the young to see that the wishes of the parents are as far as possible carried out. If this society can contribute to this great national object, it will help to keep England out of that secular current which has dragged to destruction so much of the education of other countries, which we have hitherto contrived to avoid, and which I earnestly trust we shall avoid to the last.

## 2

## On Social Reform

*Speech at a Meeting of the British Institute of Social Service, May 28th, 1914*

WE all talk about, and we all think now, of social reform. It is in the air. Everybody is considering how, in this direction, or in that direction, organised effort may improve the lot of those who require assistance. But some of us may still be under the impression that all that is required to make a successful social reformer is an abundant supply of good intentions. That really is not the case. No doubt there have been periods in which the critical spirit overshadowed the philanthropic spirit to a dangerous extent. If, indeed, you look back upon the whole school of *laissez-faire,* even in its less dogmatic beginnings, even as it is represented by such a writer as Adam Smith, you will find that the thinkers of that school admitted that there was a great deal that was wrong in our general arrangements, that there was much suffering, not that there were possible remedies by which that suffering could be diminished. They thought, however, that bad as things might be, Governments or great societies would leave things worse than they found them if they sought themselves to remedy the evils.

It was not that the world was supposed to be good, but that governmental and legislative efforts to make it better only succeeded in making it worse. You will see that doctrine stated in almost as strong terms as those in which I summarise it, in the very sober writers of a hundred, or a hundred and fifty years ago. We have altered the whole of that view, and we may have run to the other extreme. In our zeal to do the work which seems to lie at our hands waiting to be done we may have forgotten that social reform is not an easy thing, but, on the contrary, an excessively difficult thing, and that nobody can hope to be successful who does not take real trouble, not merely to invent some plausible remedy for some obvious ill, but to collect in his own country and from other countries all that experience shows can be done, or has been done in order that his own efforts may be rationally guided.

One not unimportant part of our work consists in obtaining from foreign countries accounts of what philanthropic societies or Governments within their limits try to do, and with what measure of success their efforts are attended. I believe the comparative method of philanthropy must have invaluable results. In these days when all countries are interconnected in a manner quite unknown to our forefathers, it is folly for one country to imagine that all sources of wisdom are to be found within its borders, and that nothing is to be learned from the painful and costly experience which other countries and other societies have gone through.

There is another advantage from this comparative method, an advantage which I may describe by saying that it helps the diagnosis of the evils under which we suffer. Sometimes in hasty moments of generalisation we attribute some social evil to special circumstances or special traditions of our own. Sometimes, no doubt, we may be right, but often you will find that countries where those special conditions and special traditions are not to be found, suffer from exactly the same evils. The discovery of that fact will prevent us making a wrong diagnosis of the evils with which we are concerned, for you will see that they rest upon a broader basis than merely the particular experience of a particular country, and that they are evils really incident to a particular stage in the general evolution of civilised societies. That is a most valuable result to arrive at. It prevents rash experiments. It ought not to discourage careful and sober efforts to deal with these evils as they arise.

## 3

## ON THE RELATION OF SCIENCE TO INDUSTRY

*Speech at a Conference of Research Organisations connected with the Department of Scientific and Industrial Research, December 13th, 1919*

SCIENTIFIC investigation in connection with industry is a subject in which, if I may so far be egotistical, I have always been deeply interested, and if anybody was ill-advised enough to dig into the shapeless mass of innumerable speeches which I have had to deliver on various occasions he would find a good many utterances upon this theme.

Evidently, as I think, and most of you think, the industrial progress of mankind is going to be in the near future more and more dependent upon the alliance of science and industry, and upon the co-operation of different branches of science with each other. Though we do not always act upon that principle, it has almost become a commonplace in our public discussions, though I think we are sometimes apt to forget how recent is the recognition of that truism by the general public. I do not know that there has been any book written—if so, I am not acquainted with it—on the history of the relation between industrial production and purely scientific investigations, undertaken for no other object than that of increasing our knowledge of natural law. As a matter of fact, I believe that relationship to be very recent. I hesitate to conjecture, but I think that perhaps the first of these fruitful alliances between science and practice was in connection with the discovery of Gilbert in magnetism and probably next the application of theoretical optics to the telescope and the miscroscope.

I am not going to attempt to deal with the history of this subject without more knowledge or preparation than I can give. But I think it is certainly true to say that the great industrial development in which Great Britain led the way towards the end of the eighteenth century, gave us a manufacturing supremacy over the world, which it is certainly impossible, and probably not wholly desirable, that we should ever regain. That industrial development was not in the main due to anything which pure science contributed to industry. I believe that it is partly owing to that that the great industrial community of this country, whose succession to their forefathers at the end of the eighteenth century and the beginning of the nineteenth century has not been interrupted, have not got, as it were, into the tissue of their thoughts, the idea that science is now in these days an essential element in industrial progress.

The Germans, whose industrial development came much later, have always taken a different view. I do not think that they have shown any greater aptitude for science than our fellow-countrymen, and I am sure they have shown no greater aptitude for industry; but, beginning as they did rather late in the day, with their great powers of governmental organisation, with their highly developed and equipped universities, and with the view which they have always entertained of the close alliance that ought to exist between knowledge and power, they naturally and easily did what we, with more difficulty and at a later date, are beginning to do. They marshalled, they mobilised, all the forces of science to develop their great industrial efforts.

We must not imitate them, but we must follow their example! They saw what, from the nature of the case, we could hardly be expected to see so soon, how absolutely necessary this close co-operation was, not merely in the competition of people with people, of industry with industry, but from the broader point of view that we ought to adopt if all nations were united in one great industrial community. This point of view really depends upon the consideration that it is only upon our increasing knowledge of the powers of nature that we can expect to improve the material lot of man.

One of Lord Bacon's many claims to be a great prophet of the modern movement comes from his declaration that experimental knowledge should be acquired in order to improve the unhappy lot of the human race. That is what ought to be one of the great objects for which we strive. I am not suggesting, of course, that mere material progress is all progress. I am not suggesting that either prosperity in trade or the cheapening of manufactures is going to be the great regeneration of mankind. I accept the view that "man does not live by bread alone." But to improve the material lot of man, to make the remainder of the twentieth century different from the nineteenth century, and the twenty-first century different from the twentieth is surely worth while. For this we must increase the command, for industrial purposes, which man has over the forces of nature. That can only be achieved, in the first place, by the cultivation of pure science, of science for itself, of knowledge for its own sake. It can only be achieved by striving to breed and to educate men who are consumed by a curiosity to know, without any thought of self-advancement. That end having been attained, we must learn how to apply the knowledge which they have disinterestedly acquired, to the great purposes of industrial development.

Speaking broadly, looking at the material progress of mankind, as far as we can venture on any prophecy, that, and that almost alone, is going to be the main engine of human advance.

# 4

## ON A MODERN UNIVERSITY

*Speech at the Leeds University Dinner, December 16th, 1924*

IF one looks back over fifty years to the very first inception of this University in 1874, it is impossible not to be struck with the extraordinary revolution which has taken place in our way of looking at the higher education since the great mediæval Universities were founded in this country and over the continent of Europe.

It is at once pathetic and inspiring to reflect upon the amazing enthusiasm with which men rushed to take advantage of the learning of the days in which these Universities were established. Nothing in modern enthusiasm for education can in certain respects excel the accounts that have come down to us of the way in which the mediæval students sought knowledge within the mediæval University.

But, unless I am greatly mistaken, the ideal both in mediæval times, and to a considerable extent in the times that we describe as the Renaissance, was the desire of the individual to obtain the best learning in existence, without any notion that that learning was a mere stage in the progress of humanity, and that beyond what was taught in the school there was an endless vista of scientific acquisition, still to be made—a whole unconquered continent of knowledge of which neither professor nor student had any dream. It may be said that all that was altered at the time of the Renaissance, at the time of the revival of learning, as it is called; but the mere use of the words revival of learning shows that even at that time an immense fraction of the energy of the men of learning, and of the pupils whom they educated, was devoted not so much to conquering those unknown territories as to extracting from the past the buried treasure of ancient erudition.

You will perhaps ask me why I repeat an observation, made by, I should imagine, every historian of this great University, that the earlier scheme of the Yorkshire College was on too narrow a basis. If it be true, as I have insisted, that the greatest influence in the material amelioration of the lot of man is to be found in applied science, why do I criticise the narrow foundations upon which, in its first few years, the Yorkshire College of Science was based? My reason is this: If the application of science is to be the direct source of amelioration of the lot of man, science itself, the acquisition of knowledge, cannot be pursued effectively in the spirit of wealth acquisition. If you are to have applied science, you must have pure science, because applied science is only the particular use to which pure science is devoted, and you will never get pure science to be that; it may be you will never get knowledge really furthered effectively until those who try to further it are animated in the main by the joy of augmenting knowledge in itself, rather than by considerations of the

material gains to themselves or others which their
acquired knowledge will produce.

I believe that if we had the powers of omniscient
calculation which are easily imagined but not easily
exercised, and were to compare the material rewards
which our great discoverers in pure science have
received, with the rewards which successfully applied
science brings to those who know how to use it, the
comparison would be ludicrous.

Those who have applied science have done
immense good to their fellow-creatures. On them,
I admit, depends the very existence of a community
like ours; but in many cases, at all events, their
material reward has been not inadequate to the
material gains which they have given to their fellow-
citizens. But he who pursues pure science for itself
is not often a richly rewarded member of the community. His name lives, indeed, in history. The
most undying fame is the fame of those who have
initiated some great and fertile discovery, have
opened a new vista of knowledge, have introduced
us into a wholly undreamt-of territory. But while
their spiritual reward has been great, their material
reward is not usually overwhelming in its magnitude.
They have to be content, and they may well be
content, with the admiration and the gratitude of
posterity.

Of course, it is inevitable that with the enormous
augmentation of knowledge, especially in the region
of science, you cannot avoid the curse of specialisation. I remember reading that the great Bentley,

who flourished at the beginning of the eighteenth
century, expressed the hope that he would live until
he was eighty years old, for, he said, "by the time
I am eighty I shall have read every book in every
language which is worth reading." That was a fine
boast in the mouth of that most distinguished
scholar. I do not think it was an impossible one, but
it would be obviously not merely impossible but
ludicrous at the present day, so enormously has
knowledge increased.

There is no man, whatever his acquirements, who
can suggest that he can conquer more than small
fragments of it. You perceive then, that a modern
University cannot but be in some respects at a
great disadvantage compared with its mediæval
predecessor. Their subjects of study were limited in
number. The books worth reading were even more
limited, and it was quite possible for the man of
adequate industry to master almost in detail all that
was taught at that period. It is so impossible now
that it is not even worth discussing.

How, then, can a University be a unity from the
point of view of study? I think myself that the
fact of this inevitable specialisation of knowledge is
an additional reason for making our Universities
wide in their embrace, because although students
can only devote themselves individually to a fraction
of the subject taught in their University, they are
brought into constant social intercourse with other
students pursuing their own lines of inquiry subject
to other influences. Out of that is growing that

general University culture which is of absolute necessity in modern times.

I would, therefore, say to any narrowly practical person that we shall never get an improving technique, we shall never get developing industries, unless we have pure science behind that development. Therefore you must add to that technical education in which you believe that far loftier, far more important, and far more useful foundation which pure science, and only pure science, can give.

If the practical man replies, "That may be so; I grant that a purely technical University would be a poor affair; make it embracing the circle of the sciences. Will that content you?" I say, "Certainly it will not content me, and it will not content me for the reason which I have indicated, namely, that if you simply collect together students devoted to special fractions of the sciences, if you leave arts and philosophy and theology on one side, and concentrate simply upon the one study, then though that study may be conducted with profound genius and in the most disinterested spirit, you will still fail of one essential element in those things by which the younger generation, if they are to succeed, must undoubtedly be influenced. In an ascending scale, from the narrowest to the loftiest applications of science, all hang together, all necessary one to the other, and none can be safely neglected."

I have been led by my argument, for what it is worth, into regions not perhaps very well fitted for after-dinner speaking, but they are subjects on which I feel intensely. They are subjects on which I am convinced immense service can be done, is being done, and will be done, in growing measure through the generations to come by this great University, and it is because I feel that, that I ask you to drink with enthusiasm the future of the Leeds University.

# 5

## ON THE CIVIL SERVICE

*Speech at the Opening of the Civil Service Sports Ground in Glasgow, September 18th, 1926*

I AM glad to have an opportunity of expressing in public a point of view, the importance of which, I think, is not easily to be exaggerated, but which has probably not occurred to the great mass of our fellow-countrymen. We all know what the Navy is. We all know what the Army is. We all know what the Air Force is. Do we all know what the Civil Service is?

All these four great institutions are equally servants of the State in a special sense. All of us, being citizens of the State, owe service to the State. Now the Civil Service quite obviously ranks at least on an equality with any of those three great services. If you look at it strictly, it ranks on more than an equality, because without the Civil Service it would be quite impossible for any of the three great fighting services, whose business it is to defend us, to carry out their duties and their functions had they not behind them the great organised Civil Service. I do not know how many citizens in this country quite grasp that fact or understand that the Civil Service is an organisation as much bound to public service as the Navy, the Army, or the Air Force.

I sometimes feel inclined to ask myself why that obvious truth is not realised either by the public or by the Civil Service itself? It is, no doubt, largely because the Civil Service is more scattered. It has not obviously any clear bond and functional connection with other departments in the State. To give a simple illustration, I do not think that the postman realises that he and the Ambassador are both servants of the State in exactly the same manner, and that they each, in their own departments, carry out the duties entrusted to them. I am not sure that they have that corporate sense of unity which the sailor has with the Navy or the soldier has with the Army.

But believe me, the ideal ought to be the same in all the four services. All the four services carry out functions very different in character, requiring very different training, dealing with subjects infinitely dissimilar. Nevertheless all the members of the Civil Service from the highest to the lowest should feel that they all belong to a single great organisation which owes to the State not merely the duty which every citizen owes to it, but the special duty of being the servants of the State with all that that carries with it of glorious responsibility and vital functions in the social system.

That may sound a rather abstract and doctrinaire statement, but I assure you it is not. I am speaking the actual verities of the situation as I see it. I do not think it requires to be brought to the notice of this particular audience, but I believe it does require to be brought to the notice of the public at large, and if any syllable I have said to-night travels beyond this room and meets with anything like a sympathetic echo in other parts of Scotland and other parts of the United Kingdom, I feel I shall have done a genuine service both to the public and to the Civil Service, which keeps the public in existence.

Perhaps you will say that I have travelled a little into high politics, considering that the occasion of our meeting here to-night is not politics, but football. But sport and high politics are on this occasion, in my opinion, very closely connected, and I am quite certain that such a movement serves something much greater, higher and more permanent than merely an afternoon's amusement. It will, I hope, bring home to every member of the Civil Service that he belongs to a great unity, and to every member of the general public that he belongs to a community which that great unity is ready to serve.

What we are suffering from is not that members of the Civil Service have failed in their duty. I have never been a member of the Civil Service, but my public life has brought me insistently and constantly into connection with it, and I have the profoundest admiration for the way in which they carry out their particular function in the State. I have nothing to suggest to them as individuals in regard to the manner in which they generally carry out their duty. The only thing which I think is perhaps deficient in their mind, and I am sure it is deficient in the mind of the public outside, is that this immense body of public servants is a single corporate unity, owing a single special duty to the State, and every member of it should not be content merely to carry out his own small fraction of the great duties entrusted to him, but he ought also to have a clear living consciousness of the magnitude and extent of that great body of which, in one capacity or another, he is a member.

# 6

## ON THE EFFECTS OF INDUSTRIAL DISPUTES

*Speech at the Inaugural Dinner of the Balfour Club
in Leeds, October 2nd, 1926*

I DON'T take, I think, an over-gloomy view of our position at the present time. I am an optimist, but I am an optimist who sees difficulties. Our difficulty now is that the things we can and do produce are not without rivals. On the contrary, there are competitors to be found for all we can make in every country in the world, or at all events in the great producing countries who are inevitably our competitors in the field. Let it be observed that among many of our rivals in Europe, the standard of living is lower than that which we are happy enough to possess at the moment. We therefore have to meet, in neutral markets, competition from populations adequately supplied with capital, adequately equipped with scientific knowledge, but accustomed, on the whole, to a lower standard of living.

It is absurd to say that such a position does not require a great and patriotic effort on the part of the population of this country. I don't believe for a moment that we need succumb in this competitive difficulty. But I do say that if we are going to spend our energies and our time upon industrial squabbles within the industries, we are putting ourselves in a position in this world competition which threatens us with national ruin.

It may seem that I am talking platitudes, but to appreciate the situation requires the exercise of imagination, which is rendered extremely difficult by the attitude of mind that regards all public industrial controversy as a squabble between employers and employed.

There must be differences of opinion; I do not quarrel with that.  I believe that a most valuable part may at present be performed by the trade unions, as in times past; but after all their concern is with the distribution of what is produced; their concern is properly with the question of the distribution of production.

You must have production before you can have distribution; and what is the use of squabbling about the relations between employers and employed in cases where it may even be doubtful whether there shall be production at all?

And if there is not production, or if production is seriously impaired, we are in a position worse than any other country has ever been, because we have this vast population entirely dependent not only upon what we produce, but upon what we produce and are able to sell.  That is the exact position, so far as I understand it, in which we stand.

These things are commonplaces, but they are commonplaces which should be seized by the public imagination.  We are apt to think great industrial controversies between employed and employers, in which each side suffers loss, are subjects of interest only within the industry. That is sheer folly. Who is it that suffers most from the cessation or the serious diminution of production in this country? Is it the employers in the industry? Is it merely the employed in the industry? Not in the least. That is a totally fallacious way of looking at the question. The people who suffer from these controversies, and from the loss of production which these controversies inevitably cause, are the people at large, and among them the poorest of the people. A diminution of production, however caused—whether by want of enterprise on the part of capital, or impossible demands on the part of labour—must have consequences which might fatally complicate a situation already difficult owing to the competition of other countries with a lower standard of living, but not with a lower standard of education or scientific knowledge.

I would make an appeal particularly to trade unionists. I am a very old politician, but I have never been an enemy of trade unions. The successive Conservative and Unionist Governments which I have supported, or to which I have belonged, have never shown hostility to trade unions. Trade unionism, I imagine, had practically its origin in this country; and I believe that on the whole, and under wise guidance, trade unions are a valuable element in our social and industrial life. But the leaders of trade unions, if they are to carry out the great duties thrown upon them, if they are to carry out their duty to the citizens of this country, if they are to benefit, instead of being a curse to, the future development of the country, must understand—as I am sure a very large number of them do—that their activities can only be beneficial if they face the economic facts of the situation—and nothing short of that is any good.

There is no conceivable use, nationally or morally, in merely discussing what we should like the conditions of our industry to be, unless we are prepared to face the facts of foreign competition in relation to our exports. That does not depend upon us, or upon trade union leaders. It depends upon circumstances over which no British Government has the smallest control. Yet these are among the fundamental facts which the whole community has to face, and in facing which, trade union leaders, more than anybody else in that community, must take a real, intelligent, and patriotic part. And I am sure they will do it.

# 7

## ON MODERN WAR

*Speech in the House of Lords in the Debate upon a
Ministry of Defence,\* June 16th, 1926*

MY criticism of the proposal to add to the three existing Cabinet Ministers, or to substitute one Minister for the three existing Cabinet Ministers at the
head of the Fighting Services, can briefly be stated.
It is that you ask this new Minister to do more than
any Minister can possibly accomplish, but you do
not ask him to do enough, if among his duties you
count the co-ordination of all the energies of a
country for warlike purposes. It doubly fails. The
instrument is not sufficient to carry out what you
want it to carry out—namely, co-ordination of the
three Fighting Services. No human being is capable of doing the work which would be thrown
upon him, and if he were capable of doing it he
would still leave the most important elements in
modern preparation for war quite outside his sphere
of activities. You ask him to do too much, but you
do not ask him to do enough.

That is my broad proposition. May I develop
it a little? The whole tendency of modern war-

---

\*Another aspect of this subject is dealt with in No. 7 of Section
IV on "Imperial Affairs."

like preparation is in the direction of rapid change and extreme complexity. If, for example, you will cast back your minds to the naval history of this country you might, I think, say that from the Armada, down to the invention of steam, the vital changes in the mode of fighting at sea, and in the armaments by which fighting was carried on suffered no essential change.

You may take, at the end of the sixteenth century, the Armada. At the end of the seventeenth century you may take the Battle of La Hogue. At the end of the eighteenth century you may take the Battle of the Nile, or, going a few years later, the Battle of Trafalgar. No doubt there were controversies about the proper tactics to be used in fleet actions, but, broadly speaking, manœuvring his ship and fighting his guns was what had to be done by the sailor, and it was all that had to be done by the sailor. Of course the arrangement of your fleet —whether you should cut the enemy's line, or whether you should form line ahead, or whatever it was—is a question of high tactics. But the actual way in which the fighting was carried on did not differ during the two centuries and a half to which I have referred—centuries glorious in the annals of our Navy, but centuries in which very different machinery was used for keeping the command of the sea.

Compare the present state of things with the two centuries and a half to which I have referred. Instead of its being merely a matter of bringing the ships alongside, pouring in broadsides out of smooth-bore cannons as fast as you can into the enemy's ships, you now require an amount of technical training for all your sailors of which our forefathers had no notion at all. Long range guns, torpedoes, submarines, air fighting, mines, mine-sweepers—all require different knowledge, all require a technical apparatus, which not only varies infinitely, but changes and develops with every new invention, with many scientific discoveries, with all sorts of mechanical contrivances.

I presume that the one duty of the political head of the Admiralty is to put himself in sympathy with all these various activities. They look to him to help them in all matters connected with Parliament, connected with the Cabinet, and indeed connected with their special policy. Are you going to ask any man to make himself adequately acquainted with all the intricate complexities of modern naval war, with modern land war, and modern war in the air—all the changing picture of these inventions in which one scheme of destruction, of offence, or defence, follows another with bewildering rapidity? Are you going to ask one man adequately to master that vast field of operations, and at the same time to carry on all his duties as a Cabinet Minister, as a Member of Parliament, and no doubt as an agitator through the country? Really it seems to me almost grotesque to suggest such a scheme as that.

I cannot even imagine anybody who has had any training in public affairs thinking for a moment that it is practicable. The unfortunate bearer of all these responsibilities goes to a Cabinet one day, presides over the Army Council another day, over the Board of Admiralty on a third day, over the Council of the Air Force on a fourth day. What opportunity has he got of getting to know the spirit of any one of the three Services, of making himself acquainted with their personnel, of in any sense sharing their life? He will become overloaded with responsibility, wielding in name and on paper infinite powers, but, as a matter of fact, far more impotent for any purpose of practical utility than if you gave him a third of the work to do.

Is not the whole experience of mankind against it? There is not a State in the world which mixes up its Admiralty and its War Office. If military and naval historians are to be believed, even Napoleon was not successful in grasping all the broad possibilities both of the Army and of the Navy. He knew all that could be taught about armies, but we are told that his ignorance of navies was profound, and had a very disastrous effect upon his whole policy. Well, where Napoleon failed you are not going to get the ordinary politician to succeed. Where the labours of these gentlemen are as much as any ordinary man can bear, it really is madness to multiply them by three.

There is another point which illustrates my thesis. Directly war breaks out every country finds it absolutely necessary to multiply its offices. We in this country, if I remember rightly, had ten offices by the end of the War. The French had nine. And if in war the complexities of modern operations and modern material compel you to multiply the number

of your offices, what indication is there that in time
of peace the true line of progress is that of diminishing their number?   It seems to be a quite indefensible paradox.   For that reason, I hold that the idea
of substituting a Minister of Defence for the three
heads of the three Departments is not a scheme that
any practical assembly ought to endorse.

But I have another point, which I have already
indicated.   While you ask this unhappy Minister
of Defence to do a great deal more than any man
can do, you do not ask him to do enough to co-
ordinate all your efforts in war or in preparation
for war.   Modern war differs entirely from the
wars with which in history we are familiar, in that
every single sphere of activity is called upon to
serve the great single purpose of winning the victory.

In the great wars of the eighteenth century, for
example, in which Europe and America were sometimes all engaged—they were almost world wars—
the ordinary life of the country went on very much
as it did before.   Industry, society, the general
course of social life, went on with no violent change.
The war of to-day is utterly different, largely for
the reason that we have brought in science and mechanical invention to aid us in these terrible conflicts.
If you read the Parliamentary debates of the
eighteenth century, the novels representing the
social life of the time, the newspapers, you feel at
once that, while the anxiety might be great, there
was no vital change in the direction in which human
energy was employed.   It is utterly different now.

You mobilise science, you mobilise invention, you turn your factories to purposes for which they were never intended, all your industries go in new channels, and the consequence is that the civilian side of war bears a much greater proportion to the whole energies of war than it ever did before.

The military side is but a part—I had almost been tempted to say it is not the greatest part. There is at this moment sitting a Committee looking into man power, to ascertain how man power is to be utilised with the least inconvenience to the civil population. In the eighteenth century you had a press gang, and that was all. You sent out a body of sailors, and they stole from the merchant ships a great many other sailors, and turned them into fighting men. That is all primitive and past; it all belongs to a bygone state of things. Now you have to consider questions of man power, questions of material, you have to mobilise all the intellectual resources of your country in so far as they are engaged upon science or the applications of science, your transport, your finance, your insurance—all these have to be brought in, and, without them, where would your Minister of Defence be? Your Minister of Defence depends upon them, and yet he has no control over them at all under this scheme. The idea that the Minister of Defence is a man who is responsible for all the activities which converge upon defence is to deceive yourself as to what happens when war occurs.

Was it not of Lord St. Vincent that this story was told? He went about always with a pocketful of acorns and, wherever he could see a good opportunity, he put an acorn into the ground, flattering himself that in war, if other people followed his example, England would never find herself deficient in the material for building her ships on which her safety depended. The oaks that Lord St. Vincent planted had not nearly reached their prime when an oak became the most useless thing in the world for all purposes of defence. We had substituted for oaks the most elaborate resources—the manufacture of every kind of steel, every kind of alloy, every kind of new weapon. Except for the bravery, the energy, the enterprise and the strategic capacity which is common to successful fighters in all ages, nothing could be more different than the conditions under which we fight now, and the conditions which prevailed in our forefathers' times. The difference is that you bring in the civilian in a way that you never brought him in before.

Surely the omission of any consideration of that fact entirely condemns the suggestion that by putting all the fighting forces of the country under one responsible head you would obtain that co-operation without which success is impossible. I think the argument is overwhelming. I cannot see what possible gain there would be in introducing this Minister, if you left the Committee of Imperial Defence as it is, because the Committee of Imperial Defence does the work of co-ordinating the civil and military resources of the country which no Minister of Defence could do.

The Committee of Imperial Defence has been

tried in peace and it has been tried in war. It is an institution which never, from its character, can become rigid, can never become bureaucratic. It is capable, as no other institution can be, of covering the whole ground by its Committees, dealing with questions the most disparate and the most complicated, and belonging to the most different spheres of activity. It is capable of doing all that and it is doing all that, and it seems to me that to propose anything which will lessen its utility, to do anything which will overshadow it, is to run straight counter to the avowed object of co-ordination. Co-ordination is being given us, may more and more be given us by the Committee of Imperial Defence, and I earnestly hope that with the fundamental characteristics of that body neither your Lordships' House, nor the other House, will ever desire to interfere.

# 8

## On the Need of Industry for Science

*Address to the Society of Chemical Industry on receiving the Messel Medal, July 23rd, 1926*

I NEED not tell you that the ceremony which has just been performed by the President and His Royal Highness is one which has given me, the recipient of this medal, the profoundest gratification. Of course, it would be absurd for me, in a company such as this, to make the smallest pretensions to expert knowledge of that great science, which is not merely a great science among other sciences, but which permeates the whole of life, which touches at some point or another, all the other sciences, and which has made such immense strides in recent years.

I have to admit that if quite impartially, I survey my own qualifications for this honour, I find them very defective. It is true that one member at least of my family has been very greatly distinguished in science; it is quite true that as an outside amateur, I have all my life been interested in science, that I have used such opportunities as public life has given me to further the interests of scientific research, and to utilise the immense resources of all kinds, which, in increasing measure every day, science is giving to mankind in every walk of life.

There is another qualification of an official kind which, perhaps, may have influenced the kindly judgment of those who decided to confer this great honour and distinction upon me. It is that I happen for the time being to be the head of that Department of the Government which, more than any other Department, concerns itself with industrial research.

The relation of the Government to scientific research must always be a difficult one, must always lend itself to a certain amount of controversy, and cannot be, I think, accurately embodied in any given formula. Indeed, the attempt so to embody it would only lead to pedantic difficulties, and it would be mere folly to draw too sharply the distinctions between that which the Department of Scientific Industrial Research ought to do and that which it ought not to do. The line is not precise; it must depend upon the particular exigency of the moment and the particular character of the problems that have to be dealt with, but, nevertheless, I do think it is capable of performing a very useful function in the State, and it has already, in the not numerous years of its existence, performed great services for the public.

If one reflects upon the character of the connection between science and industry it seems to me to be something, roughly, of this kind. You have men of genius, wholly unconnected with industry, moved by nothing except a desire to further knowledge, possessed of an insatiable curiosity, and with that kind of genius which enables them to penetrate a little further into the innumerable secrets of nature. To them falls the immortal glory of making those discoveries which lie at the root of all our knowledge of nature, and of all powers of turning nature to account. Their object is knowledge, but in the pursuit of knowledge they have greatly added to the intellectual and material wealth of mankind. Their discoveries are inevitably and necessarily the product of genius, which cannot be produced merely by education, which cannot be greatly fostered merely by the expenditure of money. In their efforts, which have made them among the greatest of mankind, lies the root of everything that is done, be it by subsequent investigators, be it by organised laboratories, be it by Government assistance, be it by the co-operation of great commercial organisations; they are the fathers of all our efforts, and to them, who seldom get any very great meed of this world's goods, every one of us, be his position what it may in the social organisation, owes grateful and everlasting thanks.

The next stage, perhaps, may be described as the intuition of some one of constructive ability, the intuition which enables him to see that in the discoveries made by pure science there is the foundation of some great practical application. He probably finds—I think I might go further and say that he certainly finds—obstacles in his path, obstacles of various kinds. He may, in his investigations, come upon some problem which is not, indeed, of the fundamental character of those all-embracing discoveries of which I have spoken, but which, nevertheless, affects not only his own particular line of investigation but many other collateral and allied lines.

Then, when that difficulty is overcome, the next stake would be that he attempts to test his discovery on a laboratory scale. If that effort is successful, he probably then attempts to see whether it will bear the tests of some larger effort. He makes his mechanism, a mechanism far indeed in excess, in point of size, of his laboratory experiment, but nevertheless, not amounting to the full-size scale which must be tried and tested before any scientific discovery can be directly applied to practice.

After the full-scale effort has succeeded, it may be that the next stage is that of organising a factory which contains many, perhaps, of these full-scale units, and after that there is the organisation of markets and all those collateral efforts which are required before full fruition is reached by the technical discoveries which have been made.

Of course, that is not an accurate biography of all great industrial developments, but it gives you a sort of conspectus of the kind of thing which is constantly happening. Where, in all that process, does the legitimate sphere of Government effort come in? Governments can, I think, do little, probably nothing, greatly to further the fundamental discoveries of which I have spoken as being the foundation of all the other developments. I do not think it is their business to travel to the other end of the scale; I do not think it is their business, as a rule, to find the capital which industry ought to supply for producing the full-scale apparatus or building the factories or providing for all those marketing facilities without which the best inventions of the world may prove to be fruitless. I do not say that efforts ought never to be made by a Government, but I say that broadly the centre of Governmental efforts should not concern itself with either extreme of that scale of production which I have endeavoured to describe. I think the best fields for their efforts necessarily lie in the middle regions. When you are dealing with investigations which do not affect one industry exclusively, but which might lie at the root of many industries, which are the concern of many industries, to which many industries ought to contribute, but which probably require central assistance —not, indeed, central control, but central assistance and central advice—there it may often happen that a Government may come in most usefully, and I certainly should not exclude their efforts when dealing with laboratory experiments, or the small scale experiments which follow in the kind of hierarchical ascent which I have laid before you. But when you get to that point Government assistance becomes a matter of great doubt, and should be indulged in with considerable caution. When you get to that stage it must be the enterprise of individuals or groups of individuals which must carry on to a successful financial result what has ceased to be an investigation into pure truth, and has become instead a great commercial effort, which may or may not be successful. If it is successful, the promoters will reap, as they deserve to reap, large benefits; if it be unsuccessful, they must endure with what patience

they may the losses which ineffectual effort brings
upon all of us.

Those being the functions, broadly speaking, of
the Department with which I am temporarily connected, it is inevitable that my advisers and I try
to take some general view of world industry, in so
far as it is effected by the kind of research which
I have described. If we look at the manner in which
science is applied, let us say, in Germany or in
America, and compare it with the way in which it is
applied in England, I am not sure that the results
of our investigation will prove wholly satisfactory.

If we are considering the first stage of the process, those fundamental discoveries which have
been made in extraordinary number in certain departments of science during the last quarter of a
century and more, and, indeed, if we carry our
eyes as far back as we will, I do not think we need
be ashamed of the share that this country has borne
in the furtherance of the knowledge of nature. I
am not going to argue the point. Any one of us
here may mention the names of those immortal
geniuses whose biography is a standing proof of
the accuracy of what I say, and I see no falling off,
but, if anything, the contrary, in the manner in
which, in the last twenty-five or thirty years, men
of science belonging to this country, in all departments of science, have furthered the knowledge of
these profound, fundamental, but in themselves by
no means pecuniarily profitable truths.

Nobody is going to make money, directly, for
example, out of the modern theories of the constitu-

tion of the atom. Their interest is profound; they give us a knowledge of the world in which we live, of which men of science never dreamed when I was a young man, but they are not going to fill anybody's pockets, they are not going to lead to any quotations on the Stock Exchange, and they are not going to be the parents of great dividends. In that, which, as I have said, is the foundation of any subsequent super-structure of scientific industry, I do not think we show any failure to bear our full share in the common task of civilisation, the task of furthering human knowledge of the world in which we live and human command over the resources of that world.

When we come a little lower down, when we consider how the applications of science are made, where they are best made, where they have produced the most fertile results, I must frankly own, though I do it with some feelings of discomfort, that so far as I can judge, we have not shown ourselves, and at this moment are not showing ourselves, the equal of some of our friends and competitors. I doubt whether anybody acquainted with the great scientific industries will contest what I have said. Let them only compare the number of professional chemists used in great American or German works, in a manner which must move the envy of all men living in countries where such enterprise does not attain so happy a conclusion, with the numbers used here. I do not know exactly how it is to be accounted for. Some people might be inclined hastily to suggest that this country is labouring under some disadvantage in the fact that it is very small in point of area, that it does not possess, apart from the other portions of the Empire, those material resources which, no doubt, are an essential to successful industry. But if you consider the trend of modern industrial investigation you will find that the current is running in a direction which really minimises the variety of raw material which has to be used by industry before the products of industry can reach their existing variety. A number of great commercial interests depends upon nothing more than the proper use of coal, of water, and of air; and of coal—when extracted—and of water and of air there ought to be no lack in this country whatever else we may feel the want of.

The heavy chemical industries depend more and more on coal as raw material, distinguished from coal as a source of power, light, or heat. Coal, supplemented by air and water, is more and more becoming the raw material of some of the most valuable products of human industry. The great process of synthetic ammonia, which has only come into being really since the war, is a vast and a growing industry. It ministers to the agricultural interests of every nation in the world. It is required by our own agriculture not less than by the agriculture of other people, and that great industry of synthetic ammonia requires essentially nothing except coal, water, and air. It is quite true that, as I understand the matter, sulphur is required as a vehicle for the most common form of synthetic ammonia before it can be used agriculturally, but that is an accident. It is not of the essences of the process, and I am told that the most powerful fertilisers do not use sulphur, and that they consist, therefore, of the elements which I have already enumerated—coal, water, and air.

That is a remarkable triumph of industrial development, but there are others which, in the long run, may be not less important.  I am not going to discuss technical details, but I believe that every chemist will admit the accuracy of my statement when I say that all the industries which depend upon the production of methyl alcohol, which are many, and which are growing in number and in importance, again require nothing in the shape of raw material for their production but the three things that I have mentioned—coal, air, and water.  It is an interesting reflection that out of coal, air, and water, and nothing else, you will see most valuable insulators for electrical work, and most charming handles of smart umbrellas, carved or moulded, and of admirable texture.

The fault of the public, of course, is that they know nothing whatever of science or of the resources of science, and then, when they are told that science is on the way to doing something, of making this or that great discovery, or of conferring this or that great benefit upon mankind, they always assume it is going to be done the day after to-morrow.  These things are not done the day after to-morrow, but they are done in time, and I do not doubt that sooner or later, and it may be sooner, we shall see these great developments which again will show how enormously this country, poor as it may seem in a certain variety of raw material, has, nevertheless, the kind of raw material to which chemical industry can go for variety and can turn to every sort of account, and, by all the magic of organic chemistry, can give us products of the most varied kind, from dyes and medicines to heavy oils, and light oils, and so on, and thereby immensely further not merely the prosperity of great corporations, not merely the employment of vast numbers of workers, but will add directly to the comfort of every single individual within our narrow and crowded frontiers.

These are considerations which, for those who look at the material side of civilisation—not a side by any means to be despised—are of a satisfactory and hopeful description. From our point of view, however, they are rather disquieting, because every one of the inventions to which I have referred is of foreign origin. That ought not to be. It has no justification, as I said earlier, in the indifference of our countrymen to scientific pursuits or their failure to attain great triumph in those pursuits. Of that there is no question. Evidently there is something in the way we organise the relations between practical industry and the scientific results which I have described as middle results which requires our serious consideration. It is incredible that in these new industries the Americans and the Germans should require the services of chemists, not necessarily men of genius, but competent, well-trained chemists, in numbers incomparably greater than those used by ourselves. It must be wrong, because not only does the inadequate use of the human scientific material which we have at our disposal greatly injure us in the discovery of new processes, but it does a great injury in maintaining a process when once discovered.

A process, once it is working, once it is bringing in profits to the manufacturer and providing wages for the workmen, is not a self-sustaining, an immutable process.  It requires perpetual improvement and adjustment, it must be buttressed up by new discoveries, perhaps small discoveries in themselves, but, in their cumulative effect, of enormous importance in world competition.  All those things require, and ought to have, an immense body of trained and competent technical assistants.  I am not sure that even in places of high authority in great industries we use the best scientific knowledge to the best advantage.  I am quite sure that we do not use the second best, the more ordinary, more easily obtained, more familiar technical competence in adequate quantities.  The result is that in our modern industries we find it difficult, and in some cases we find it impossible, to hold our own against our competitors, not because we have any material disadvantages to contend with, but because, in some respect or another, we do not use to the best advantage the human resources which are in such large measure at our disposal.  I am certain that, to conduct great modern developments of industry—I use the word "developments" with intention—the managers of businesses must have not only ability and probity— those we possess in abundance—but they must have also a sense of imagination. They must see how profoundly important it is that we should not merely be conducting our business with skill, honesty, efficiency, liberality to our workpeople, and all the other industrial virtues, which I think we can command, but that we must have some foresight, some imaginative power of looking into the future. The future that we look into—please remember it—must be a future moulded by scientific knowledge; if we lack either the imagination or the knowledge, we cannot help being at a disadvantage with those who are possessed of both.

I hope you will not suppose that I am making an attack on the great business community of this country. Very far from it. I yield to none in my admiration of their business capacity, of their incomparable directness and honesty, and of the modern intellectual qualities which have given them a special place in the economic working of the world. I do think that they are in some respects, and in some quarters, lacking in that combination of special scientific knowledge with a broad and imaginative scientific outlook, which is more or less possessed by some great industrial countries with whom we are brought into the closest relations, not merely of friendship but of competition.

I have perhaps pressed too much on the industrial side of chemical industry. Do not think for a moment that it is the only side which I value. I hope, indeed, that what I said earlier will convince you that I do not look at the study of science from a merely material or financial point of view. Very far from it. The greatest of all the aspects of scientific study is the discovery of how the world we live in is constructed, what its real intimate character is. We cannot penetrate all its secrets; that is a hope which none of us need entertain. But when I reflect upon how much has been done by chemistry and by the sciences closely allied to chemistry, whether on the physical or on the biological side, within my own relatively recent memory; when I contemplate the undoubted fact that our outlook on the material world has really profoundly changed in the course of one generation; and when I remember how much of that work has been done by our countrymen (although I am far from suggesting that science should be regarded from the narrowly national point of view), and when I see that we are not now in the forefront of industrial investigation, and that from some points of view we cannot even think of ourselves as in the forefront of practical manufacture, then it does seem to me that when men with technical knowledge of their subject meet together, they may perhaps think of some of the things which I have ventured to lay before you, and come to the conclusion that no adequate remedy can be applied to the evils except by the industries themselves, and by the full realisation by all those who conduct those industries, that if they are to keep their place in the modern world they must make a profound and imaginative study of modern science.

# 9

## ON THE HUMAN SIDE OF INDUSTRY

*Speech in support of the National Institute of Industrial Psychology, May 5th, 1927*

WE are all impressed with the obvious necessity that when we are dealing with modern industrial conditions and modern machinery we should have experts acquainted with that machinery and intimately concerned with all the principles which underlie its working.  Upon their advice, the manufacturer lays out his plant; the maker of machinery constructs his machine; and the result is no doubt an admirable factory with admirable machinery embodying the latest results of scientific research.  But though never denied, it has really never been formally or explicitly explained to all those concerned, that machines inevitably require men to work them, and that it is quite as essential to consider the human side, as it is to consider the mechanical side.  They work together; the total results are due to their joint effort; and the idea that one may be neglected, working as it were of itself without the scientific investigation which you give to the other, is surely a mistake.

Now I am not suggesting for a moment that the managers and overseers are lacking in humanity.

I do not think they are, and if you said to them, "You have to consider the welfare of those in your employment and those who collaborate with you in the work of production," they would gladly assent. But if you said to them, "Now you have got all the best experts you can, to settle the character and the arrangement of your machinery, and all the methods by which production is increased. Yet you do nothing scientifically with regard to the other half of the productive process," I think they would reply, "That is not a matter to which we have ever given consideration."

Now, I hope, consideration will more and more be given to this matter. It is all-important. It deals with industry; and the world depends increasingly upon industry. It has to do with the smooth working of your industrial machine; and more and more the world depends upon your industrial machine. Surely it must be with a sigh of relief that we turn to a subject dealing with industry, dealing with employers and employed, which raises no bitterness of controversy—a subject on which employers and employed are alike agreed. Whenever they take advantage of the scientific investigations which we desire to place at their disposal, all express their gratitude; the employer finds that those he employs are more successful in production, and the employed finds the conditions of employment easier and more satisfactory.

We are, after all, particularly concerned in a task which is one of the most important that lies before those who are engaged upon social reform, and that is the complete explosion of the superstition that all our hours of work are a minus quantity in the happiness of life, and all the hours of idleness are plus ones. That is a most ludicrous and pernicious doctrine, and its greatest support comes from our not taking sufficient trouble, not making a real effort, to make work as near pleasure as it can be. I do not wish to put this too high. I am a great lover of idleness. I am always glad to hear that there are some hours of the day in which no one is going to ask me to do anything. Yet, after all, if you were to segregate one hundred children, or one hundred adults for that matter, into two halves of fifty, and say to one half, "You shall work your eight hours a day steadily, week in or year in, and week out or year out," and say to the other half, "You shall never do anything," then those who were ordered to do nothing would certainly commit suicide before the experiment had lasted very long. But I will not go further into that.

Here is a sphere of activity in which employers and employed have not only common interests, but have manifestly the same interest. I believe that the work we are doing in their common interests, wherever it has been carried out, has produced gratitude on both sides. But that deals with only half of the energies of our Institute—with human nature and the average human being. There is another side of our work which recognises that while there is an average of human capacity and human energy, there are individual differences which it is of importance, if possible, to consider in the division of labour among the individuals of the community. To that also this Institute has devoted itself.

How far this branch of the work can be expanded, to what degree the community can be ranged so that occupation and capacity shall to some extent fit in, I cannot say. But I am sure that it is to a great extent worth striving for, and I think the degree to which the Institute has already striven has produced considerable fruits.

SECTION IV
ON IMPERIAL AFFAIRS

On Mr. Joseph Chamberlain and the Empire

*Speech on receiving the Freedom of the City of Birmingham, June 23rd, 1922*

Frankly, when I come to Birmingham to receive the highest honour which that great city can bestow, it is not upon any work of my own that my thoughts dwell, but upon the work of the one who in the whole Roll of Honour of the honorary citizens of Birmingham stood first and greatest—my friend, Mr. Joseph Chamberlain. The Roll of Honour contains not many names. The city has been chary of bestowing its freedom. Among those names the majority are those citizens who have deserved well of that great community.

There are a few—not more than four—whom you have asked to accept the honour, who have had no connection with the local interests of Birmingham, with the great work which had made the Municipality of Birmingham the very model of what energetic citizenship could accomplish. Those four names are: Lord Roberts, the Prime Minister of Australia and last, but not least, my immediate predecessor in the reception of the honour, the present Prime Minister of the country. Great indeed is the honour of being the fourth on that list. But it is to the man who headed the list who both represented the very spirit and essence of municipal self-government and, at the same time, had his name unalterably and eternally connected with one of the greatest movements of development of the British Empire—it is to Mr. Joseph Chamberlain that our thoughts turn when we meet for such a ceremony as that in which we are now engaged.

Some have thought that the absorption in the common work of municipal life stunts the wider imagination and renders a man little capable of taking in the greater problems of the world outside the community in which his work particularly lies. I believe that to be a profound mistake. My own personal conviction is that the man who shows himself capable of really grasping the meaning of co-operate effort of all classes, embracing all local ends—is the man most capable of seeing the true proportions and character of the great problems which lie beyond the immediate works in which he is engaged.

Whether that generalisation is true or not, it certainly was true so far as Mr. Joseph Chamberlain was concerned. It was on his municipal work in Birmingham that he first founded his enduring reputation, and he made that the basis on which were constructed all the great imaginative schemes to which the later years of his public life were devoted. I do not suggest for a moment that the British Empire was the work of one man or of one party. The British Empire was, to its glory, the natural out-growth of the efforts of men of all creeds, of all political views, sharing, perhaps, nothing but a common patriotism. Yet, although the work of developing our great self-governing Empire has found contributors on all sides and in all parties, I think that in the cool atmosphere of future ages the historian of these great and critical times will write the name of Mr. Joseph Chamberlain before that of any other statesman directly connected with organising this great new community of free States.

Mr. Chamberlain's loss was one of infinite magnitude not merely to his party, to his city, to his country, or to the Empire. Mourning the loss of a great man and a great friend, mourning also that he did not live thoroughly to see and appreciate in the course of the Great War, the magnitude of the work of which he had borne so great a share, the solidity of the work of which he was one of the master masons.

Let us remember what those severe critics, our enemies, thought of the British Empire before the war. If, in the early months of 1914, one had asked a German statesman to remember that if they provoke a war on the Continent of Europe, they would probably drag in Great Britain; they would certainly also drag in those great self-governing communities which shared with Great Britain the glory of making up the British Empire, he would probably have replied: "It is quite true that if you look at the map of the world no insignificant part of it is coloured red; that there are vast continents, vast areas in America, a whole continent in the Pacific, vast regions in Asia, to say nothing of smaller Colonial possessions, and these have an imposing appearance. But what worth will they be under the strain and stress of a great war? Are the British Dominions, divided from the theatre of war by thousands of miles of stormy sea, going to sacrifice their citizens, to expend their wealth, in supporting this small island in the northern seas in its attempt to preserve the liberties of Europe? No," he would have said; "from that danger, at all events, the German Empire is free. We may have to count with the British islands. With the British Empire, we shall not have to count."

That was the prophecy, and from the unimaginative standpoint of the prosaic German attempting to count up by a shallow arithmetic the motives that animated mankind, was it a bad calculation! It was extremely plausible. But, thank Heaven, it was utterly untrue. This Empire, which Mr. Chamberlain did so much in building up, stood the stress of the greatest war that has ever been seen, far better than some of the countries which lay within the theatre of operations, and the result has been a victory of right over wrong, of international freedom over international slavery.

Well, after all the tremendous efforts through which the Allied and Associated Powers went between 1914 and 1918, a reaction was inevitable. It was inevitable in this case, because, perforce, every component part of the Empire found itself under the hard necessity of repairing the injuries and losses which this tremendous struggle involved, and of restoring itself to a position of prosperity and peace. Now is the time to consider what the past has given us, and what remains for us in this connection in the future.

The past has done two things at least. It has shown of what fibre the tissue of the British Empire is composed. It has also performed a wonderful task in organising the States of which the Empire is composed. Before the War these developments were led up to by Imperial Conferences which produced the most valuable results, but it was during the war, in the stress and agony of a great conflict, that the Prime Ministers of these States met together in France, or at the heart of the Empire in Downing Street, under the conditions of secrecy, confidence, mutual trust, in which a Cabinet discusses matters within the area of its responsibility.

I do not believe we can yet measure the benefits that this is beginning to have in the Empire. We have actually been in process during the last thirty years—some of us do not quite realise it—of making a wholly new experiment in free government. The English-speaking nations are the authors of the greatest and most successful experiment in free government. It is to us, to the efforts of our forefathers, to the dwellers in this small island, that the first model of a modern free state is really due. It was of slow growth; it was a growth whose beginnings were lost in the mists of antiquity. The second great experiment was that which was made by men of our own speech and traditions when the citizens of thirteen States in America turned them into a single free self-governing community, and I doubt whether the majority of the people in this country realised how difficult and how necessary that task was.

It has been my privilege to discuss this very problem with the Solicitor-General for America. He brought out the condition of complete, hopeless, chaos and anarchy in which the thirteen States found themselves after their successful war with this country, and before they had seen their way to organise themselves into one great State. That work was the work of the authors of the American Constitution, and nobody could judge of its magnitude or greatness unless they thoroughly realised the conditions in which it was undertaken. That was the second great experiment made by men of our speech and race in the task of framing great and free institutions.

The third is one very different from either of those in which Mr. Chamberlain played a great part—one not yet fully accomplished. It is that of welding together States having a common ancestry, common laws, common modes of thought, common institutions, but which are separated by thousands of miles of ocean. These States are self-contained, have their special social and economic problems, and, unlike the thirteen States of America, are not contiguous or undivided by natural obstacles. The problem we have to solve is how finally to organise into some complete and perfect form these communities without interfering with their freedom and without loss of that sense of unity and the necessity on great occasions of making a common effort, which is the very strength and life-blood of the Empire.

I have been tempted to go very far from the immediate purpose of this meeting. I cannot, however, regret it, for I feel frankly that, speaking in this Town Hall and in this city, I should utterly fail to do justice to my own feelings if I were not to make my principal theme the contribution of Mr. Chamberlain to that which must be the greatest cause and the one nearest to our hearts. I stand here, I think the oldest surviving Cabinet colleague of your great citizen, and rejoice to think that the city with which his name was inseparably connected has thought fit, travelling entirely outside personal or political consideration, to confer upon me the honour which it first conferred on Mr. Chamberlain.

## On Inter-Imperial Relations

*Speech in the House of Lords, December 8th,*
1926

I was reminded to-day of a speech which, frankly, I had quite forgotten, that I myself made in your Lordships' House, which appears to me to put the whole case. I said in reference to the relations between the Mother Country and the Dominions:

"My own personal view is that the relations are those necessary for equality. None of us conceive that of this conglomeration of free States one is above the other. One may have more responsibility than another, one may be in more dangers than another, one may be closer to the centre of international complications than another, but all are on an equality. That is the very essence, as I understand it, of the British Empire. As to exactly what that equality involves, as to exactly what degree of responsibility each has for the other, on that I personally think very little is gained by refining, discussing, or defining."

May I read what follows, because it deals with another point:

"I should say that so far as this country is concerned we are bound to go to war to defend any part of this Empire which is in danger. Personally I think the duties of all the other members of the Empire to us are not less than our duties to them, but, as to the particular conditions under which that great duty is to be exercised, I do not believe anything is gained by inventing hard cases beforehand."

That is what I said a month before the Imperial Conference met. It is what, equally strongly, at the moment, I believe.

We stand on an equality, and if some foreign critics are disposed to say that standing on an equality means that we are bound to separate in a short time, my view is precisely the contrary. My view most strongly is that the British Empire is now a more united organism than it has ever been before, that that organism is held together far more effectually by the broad loyalties, by the common feelings and interests—in many cases, of history—and by devotion to great world ideals of peace and freedom.

A common interest in loyalty, in freedom, in ideals—that is the bond of Empire. If that is not enough, nothing else is enough.

I can perfectly understand any political theorist saying ten years ago that the British Empire was of all political fabrics the feeblest and the least efficient for any purpose of offence or defence or mutual support. But how anybody can think that after the War seems to me perfectly amazing. It may well be that after the War some people may have said to themselves: "Well, one result of the War is that a great many communities have been

dragged into it who might have been kept out of it."
But that is not the prevailing feeling that has been
left. Nothing, as I believe, can increase the feeling
of solidarity more than the sense that that solidarity
depends on the complete sense of free equality.

There cannot be, of course, equality of function
in this Empire. That must depend on the circumstances of the moment. At the moment, and for
many, many years to come, the main burden of
defence must necessarily fall upon this country. For
many years to come—perhaps for an indefinite
period—owing to our geographical position, the leading part, and at present by far the most important
part, of the conduct of our foreign affairs must also
fall on this country. But these are questions of
function varying with the conditions of the time,
varying with the actual practical necessities that
have to be met. They in no way conflict with that
fundamental equality of status which can be the only
permanent bond between these self-governing portions of the Empire.

I do not, of course, deny that the position of the
Dominions in relation, for example, to the League
of Nations carries with it anomalies. That had
nothing to do with the Conference. That had to do
with the obvious facts of the case, with the War,
with the Peace, with the signing of the Treaty,
with all those great events which have hastened the
movement that reached a culmination in the Resolu-
tions of the Conference that has just separated.
But the Conference did not create those difficulties,
the laws of England did not create them, and if inter-

national law has not the sense to get over them, we must manage as best we can.

The fact remains and will, I hope, always remain, that these self-governing States of which the Empire is composed have each a separate identity which, I think, could not but be recognised after the events of 1918, and that the difficulties of that separate identity, in which we are all equal, in which this country has no superiority over any one of the Dominions, will be got over in practice. It is got over at every meeting in Geneva. I am sure that my noble friends and I could have invented any number of hard cases when we had these co-equal, self-governing communities all represented on the League of Nations, and all able by their separate veto to stop the League of Nations doing anything. You would say *a priori* that this was a system that would not work at all. I am not prepared to say that it will never produce a difficulty, but I do say that it has worked perfectly up to the present moment, and that my belief is that the common-sense of other nations and the patriotism and the feeling of unity of the separate members of the Empire will enable it to work successfully in the future as it has so far successfully worked in the past.

# 3

## On the Evolution of the Empire after the Imperial Conference of 1926

*Speech, at Edinburgh, January 27th, 1927*

It is with great pleasure that I respond to the invitation to speak on a subject which, though entirely non-controversial, profoundly interests every citizen of the British Empire. I think the whole community has been conscious, after the issue of the Conference Report, that an important moment had been reached in the evolution of the British Empire. But what exactly was done by the Conference I think they were not quite so clear about, and that was most natural, because, in the first place, they were well aware that the Conference, august though it was, consisting of the Prime Ministers of all the self-governing Dominions and of Great Britain, had no legislative power, had no power of altering laws which govern the Empire, or, indeed, of doing anything at all except give advice in their respective Dominions to the Parliaments by whose support and faith they were present at Westminster.

What, then, was the change that had taken place? The reply was far from obvious, because it never had been denied, for many, many years, that the Dominions were autonomous. It had been explicitly stated by persons in authority, not, indeed, in any very formal fashion, but—what was even more impressive than a formal statement—it had been stated in the course of speeches as an accepted fact, before audiences which would certainly have expressed objection had they entertained doubts on the subject.

I myself remember when I was Prime Minister incidentally making a speech on another subject in which I asserted as a universally accepted fact that the Dominions were autonomous, and that the idea of any Government in Great Britain interfering with that autonomy was, in fact, unthinkable, and I was reminded that I made a similar statement on the subject at the Albert Hall three years before the War.

Now, why do I say three years before the War? I say it because the War was a crucial incident in the whole recent development of the Empire. It was, as I believe, the accepted fact, though never stated in any formal writing, that the self-governing Dominions were autonomous in the fullest sense of the word. Many persons were quite ready to take account of that, and they immediately drew the moral, especially foreigners, that if the British Empire was simply a collection of autonomous States, with no central authority, bound together by no compulsory laws, why, then, it was not an Empire at all, and whatever airs it might give itself and however it might talk of our far-flung Dominions, in fact it was a loosely constructed political entity that did not count as a great world force either for war or for peace.

Well, whether it counted for war or not was soon

settled in the eyes of the world. To the dismay of
our enemies and the delight of our friends, the
British Empire, when the time of trial came, showed
itself as powerful for purposes of Imperial defence
as the most highly organised military despotism of
which history gives us any record, and undoubtedly
the British Empire has shown what it could do as
a unity, although largely composed of those autonomous portions.

There was still a lesson to learn. The War
taught the unity of the Empire for the purpose of
defence.  The peace came, and again that very
unity, which had been so manifest when the Empire
was in danger, showed itself as a unity composed
of independent parts when the moment came for
settling the terms of peace.  All through those fate-
ful months when the terms of peace were under
discussion, we were in the closest touch with our
colleague from the Dominions in Paris, and when
the time for signing the final Treaty of Peace came,
every separate Dominion signed as an independent
Power.  Never was that unity and diversity in unity
shown in clearer terms before the face of rather an
astonished and puzzled world.

At this moment, when at Geneva the League of
Nations meets, the representatives of the Dominions
go there, of course, on equal terms with every other
nation.  Although, as a matter of arrangement
among ourselves, the representatives of the Empire
are in constant and friendly communication in
Geneva, all their constitutional power, as Members
of the League, are identical with the constitutional

powers of any other State in the world, from the greatest to the smallest.

Now, if that is so, and if it was so before the Conference of 1926, what, you may perhaps ask, was there for the Conference to do? In the first place, I think this absolute equality of status was perhaps more obvious to the home country than it was to one or two at least of the Dominions.

In the second place I would remind you that the Empire in its present condition is the result of an evolutionary process, in which law has always lagged behind practice. There is a well-known and admirable book called "The Law and Practice of the Constitution." I am not sure that the title would not have been more appropriate to the actual development of Great Britain, and the Empire to which Great Britain belongs, if the title had been "The Practice and Law of the Constitution." I won't argue about that. I will only point out that considering that what are now the Dominions were originally, for the most part, small and powerless communities dependent on the Mother Country for many things besides protection, in every sense children, and at that time with the status of children —of course, English-speaking people being what they are, it was inevitable that as they grew, their whole position altered, and that, though no doubt the laws under which they worked gradually changed, the actual position of the law was always behind the actual practice.

It must now be a quarter of a century since perfectly explicit statements have been made, without contradiction, of the absolute equality of status between Dominions and Mother Country. But though that represents the facts and the practice, it does not in all respects represent the actual statute law, which the learned among you may find buried away in Acts of Parliament. And of course, if and when there was in any particular Dominion a section of the community who, according to the practice of sections of the community in free countries, were very glad to pick holes in anything that was done by their political opponents, these survivals of a defunct practice were all dragged to the front and were made the topic of criticisms of the Dominion status, all implying that the status was unfair to the status enjoyed by the Mother Country.

That was never held here, never, I believe, by thinking people. It was held by many, perhaps, in certain of the Dominions, and it was all-important that when the Prime Ministers met together last November, they should singly and severally, in their collective, as well as in their private, capacity, give their great authority to what we in this country have long believed to be a true doctrine—the doctrine of equality of status. I think that was a very great and vital stage in Empire-building.

There was another doctrine, less important, but worth formulating, and which, so far as I am aware, has never been formulated until a very few weeks or months ago. It is this—that while for all time the status of those autonomous members of the British Empire is identical, there is, and there must be, a differentiation of function. It must be that to one of these Dominions should be entrusted the leading part, let us say, in diplomacy—the leading part in the organisation of defence.

All the Dominions are brought in counsel, all the Dominions are kept informed, as far as conditions of time and space permit, of what is going on, of what is passing in the minds of those conducting our affairs here, of their views. Also, of course, any opinion from any Dominion receives the full weight to which it is entitled, but some differentiation of function there is, always has been, and, I think, always must be. It is not merely that to Great Britain has been entrusted the leading part in diplomacy and defence, but Australia, for example, has a special function with regard to one of the Mandated Territories; New Zealand has a special function with regard to another, and South Africa is responsible for the Mandated Territory of German South-West Africa.

So that is the system which exists, that is the system which ought to exist; I don't say ought to exist in its present shape for all time. I do say that equality of status exists, but the actual arrangement of such differentiation of function as I have indicated must be subject naturally to variations of form as variations of circumstance require or suggest.

Now the great technical importance, the formal importance of the Conference of 1926, is that all the representatives of these great Dominions—and our own Prime Minister is one of them—have met round a table, and have, in face of all the world, declared both the fundamental doctrine of equality of status, and the somewhat different, but not unimportant, corollary that, though there is equality of status, that must be associated with some differentiation of function. That is all I have to say about what I may call the formal side of this great development.

I should like to say something upon a side that is in some respects far more important. Call it moral, emotional, sentimental, historical, or what you will, I mean that we should look at this problem from the standpoint of those who look behind and look in front, and who try to forecast the future of that great institution to which formal expression was given in December last.

You may ask me whether, having roughly explained what I conceive to be the Constitution of the self-governing portions of the Empire, I think it the best possible Constitution that could be contrived. The question is, in my opinion, an idle question, because the Constitution now formally declared is absolutely the only Constitution which is possible if the British Empire is to exist, and we need not argue whether it would not be better to have a central authority, whether some means of coercion in extreme cases ought not to be contrived.

All this constitution-mongering is utterly out of place when you are dealing with the natural growth of the British Empire, and when you remember that the Empire is scattered in fragments in every part of the habitable globe. It was possible for the framers of the American Constitution to give State rights and to combine with maintenance of State rights a central authoritative Government. But America, large as she is, is on one continent. We are scattered in every continent, and it would be quite impossible for us in any sense to copy or to imitate the great work that was done by the English-speaking inhabitants of North America after the separation from the Mother Country.

I myself, however, do not regard the absence of a central authority with the kind of fears that assail those who are brought up upon legal considerations, and who put emotional considerations on one side. I do not, of course, deny the importance of central authorities where you can have them. I should like to feel that every person of British blood could consult in some Chamber, through his immediate representatives, with regard to everything affecting the Empire, but that you cannot do and never will be able to do. I will not admit, however, that though we are deprived of that great advantage, we must inevitably describe ourselves as having to be content with the second best.

You may ask if I am not exaggerating the power of sentiment as a binding force. Remember, my imaginary critic might say, that some of the memories of some of our great Dominions are not entirely connected with matters in which there has been no controversy between this country and their predecessors. If memory is to be the foundation of your future greatness, are your memories always so satisfactory that they will supply a solid foundation for such a future? Well, I am a Scotsman addressing Scotsmen, and I feel, therefore, peculiarly qualified to speak on this subject. I maintain, and I appeal to the history of my country to show that I am right, that these different traditions can well be united in one whole; that although these different streams which have met together to make our kingdom and our Empire, may have flowed from different sources, none of them need feel that that difference destroys the unity of the stream which has resulted from their coalescence. I absolutely refuse to allow any man, be he English or be he Scottish, to rob me of my share in Magna Charta and Shakespeare because of Bannockburn and Flodden. What we have done, all can do. We can look back without shame, and we can look forward with unbroken hope.

Personally, I hazard what some may think the paradoxical opinion that this creation of the British Empire is the final crown of the endeavours, the half-conscious endeavours, which we in these islands have made for centuries. All our greatest work has been, as it were, done unconsciously, done not in the spirit of system-makers, but in the spirit of dealing from moment to moment with the necessities of the moment. The English, without really knowing what they were doing, invented Parliaments. The Scottish, without really knowing what a lesson they were giving, were the first to show what democratic patriotism could do in the very height of the Middle Ages and the feudal system. The subjects of George III, when they had thrown off allegiance to the British Crown, set themselves to work, and on the basis of the liberties which they had inherited from our common forefathers, built up a Constitution which has shown itself equal to dealing with the unforeseen magnitude of the problems which must face so vast a territory, governed by so energetic a population.

We are the direct descendants and brothers of those who made this great and unique performance. No other nation has done anything like it at all. We, through the force of circumstances, without conscious premeditation, in no character of constitution makers, find ourselves members of an Empire based on principles hitherto wholly unrecognised in the past, without any example, and yet, I think, in a spirit which looks forward to the future in hope and in belief.

I do not tell you that the task before us is an easy one. I do not tell you, or any of our brother-subjects of the King in other Dominions, that, though this has been laid down in black and white at a Conference in 1926, their labours are over. Their labours are just begun. I would not lay down the positive assurance that the future even of Parliamentary institutions, elsewhere or in this country, is absolutely safe. But I do say that the experiment we are trying is a result of a natural development, that it has that great security behind it; and I am confident that the patriotism, common-sense, the instinctive looking to the past, and working for the future which have been the characteristic of the English-speaking peoples, are going in the future to bring to a successful issue one of the noblest experiments mankind has ever tried.

# 4

## INTRODUCTION TO THE REPORT OF THE RESEARCH SPECIAL SUB-COMMITTEE OF THE IMPERIAL CONFERENCE, 1926

*(By the Right Hon. the Earl of Balfour, K.G., O.M., F.R.S., Lord President of the Council and Chairman of the Research Special Sub-Committee.)*

THE material well-being of mankind may be diminished by many causes—e.g., international wars, domestic disorders, industrial disputes—but (if individual effort remain on the average unchanged) there are only two causes which can increase it—namely, better natural sources of supply, and better methods of turning these sources to account. If we are to reply (as we increasingly must) on the second of these causes of economic progress, it is to applied science that we must turn for aid.

But, granting this to be true, how, it may be asked, does the fact concern the Imperial Conference?

It concerns the Imperial Conference because we are here touching on interests that are more than regional. The Empire includes States and territories of the most varied economic capacity; possessing every gradation of climate and soil, every species of mineral wealth, subject in parts to special diseases with which only science can hope to deal;

enjoying in parts unique natural advantages which only science can fully develop. It possesses distinguished investigators in every branch of research. It has therefore everything to gain from full scientific co-operation, yet we can hardly flatter ourselves that we practice this, either within Great Britain or throughout the Empire. Here, surely, we find ourselves face to face with a situation in which the free discussions of the Conference may give us priceless aid.

But what, it may be asked, can such discussions really accomplish? Doubtless the relations between science, industry, and departmental administration are far from easy; but would they not become wholly impossible if even the faintest attempt were made to improve them through any form of Imperial control? They certainly would; and it is not in this direction that better co-operation is to be looked for.

Again, can we suppose that either money or organisation can increase the supply of original scientific genius, or direct it, when found, into utilitarian channels? It is plainly impossible. Genius cannot be made to order, nor discovered by rule. The best we can do is to provide fitting opportunities for its exercise when we are fortunate enough to find it.

These may seem to be discouraging reflections; yet I am convinced that much may be accomplished if we are not too ambitious. To make the position clear let me roughly sketch the four stages into which we may ideally divide the reactions of science on particular industries.

They begin with the fundamental discoveries in pure science on which all subsequent progress depends. These have commonly been made with no thought of any useful application, and are due to the love of knowledge alone.

The second stage is reached when it occurs to some man of science that these fundamental discoveries may be employed in the solution of a practical problem which has been engaging his attention.

The third stage (which is closely associated with the second) consists in exploring the full significance and value of this conjecture by means of small scale experiments, while

The fourth consists in the application of the knowledge thus obtained to the business of economic production.

Such in bare outline seems to be the normal movement from fundamental discoveries to the most advanced enterprises of the agriculturist and the manufacturer. In historic fact it is often a very long and very elaborate journey, filled with dramatic complications, sometimes even with dramatic tragedies. About these we are not concerned; for it is on the two middle stages of the process that the efforts of organised research are chiefly concentrated; and we may almost say that their principal aim is to shorten and cheapen the passage which separates pure scientific theory from pure industrial practice.

There are at this moment in different parts of the Empire a large and increasing number of Institutions devoted to this purpose, and the work they are individually doing is admirable in quality, and as large in quantity as their financial resources permit.

How then is it possible for the Conference to assist? It cannot give money; it cannot impose a policy. The greatest service it can render (and it may be no small one) is to encourage those States of the Empire which are interested in research to consider sympathetically the suggestions contained in this Report. Those who do so will probably agree with the conclusion I have ventured to indicate. Let us cultivate easy intercourse, and full co-operation will follow. Investigators in the same intellectual field, though far separated in space, will work as partners. Overlapping, and all the intellectual waste that so often accompanies overlapping, will be greatly diminished; and considered judgments about the gaps in our knowledge which most urgently require to be filled will follow as of course.

# 5

## On Imperial Aspects of Scientific Research

### Speech at the Dinner of the Royal Society of Tropical Medicine and Hygiene, 1926

IF I try to look at the scientific movement which is going on before our eyes in its Imperial aspects and in connection with the other public activities of the most advanced nations, I am profoundly struck by the growing closeness and intimacy between all these forms of human activity. It is not many years ago—within my own lifetime—that, while nobody would pretend that the spheres of human activity were wholly separate, in practice they were separate; in practice the man of science was either a physicist or an astronomer or a chemist—I do not think the word "biologist" was very fashionable then; but each was concerned with a separate department of human knowledge, and to that he devoted, with admirable results, the activities of his lifetime, without being forced to consider, as we are forced to consider, how intimately all those activities are connected together.

If you take the African problem, for example, and if you start with the economic aspect presented by Africa at the present moment, I suppose that a hundred years ago all that people asked themselves was: What trees, what crops, what minerals did Africa produce which had a ready sale in the London market, or in countries which probably were financed by the London market? That was all that was asked.

The administrator asked himself: "How can I creditably govern this state, a huge area with black men, which has been entrusted by the British Government to my charge?"

Those problems and many others were regarded separately. If you sent out a doctor and he was a man of observant habits he came back with useful knowledge, but these matters were not considered in their inter-relation. In these days it is impossible to avoid considering them in any other way than in their inter-relation. If you want to make an economic success of Africa you must study biology, botany, physics, medicine, and so on; if you try to omit one of them you will see what happens at once —you will fail in some serious aspect of the work which has been set before you.

Anthropology, indeed, has taught us, I believe, the need for studying matters in a more effective manner. I was looking only the other day at one of the papers presented to this Society by a Fellow, in connection with Melanesia, and I found the author was entirely interested in the scientific aspect of things, and pointed out how great was the loss of life owing to the ignorance of the anthropology of those races on the part of those who, as a matter of fact, had to govern them and to influence them. And what is true of Melanesia is undoubtedly equally true of Africa.

I am not going to discuss anthropology, but it is

quite clear that I chose that science because it could be regarded as the most remote of all from the economic and administrative work which is plainly and obviously thrown upon us. If it is true, as I have just contended, that all these things are, now, in the light of modern knowledge, becoming more inter-connected every day, how are we going to deal with a problem of this increasing complexity?

I do not think we have arrived at a solution of that problem yet, but anybody who follows, for example, what occurred at the Inter-Imperial Conference, will agree that that section of the Conference which had entrusted to it the consideration of these research problems, showed the keenest appreciation of the necessity of growing inter-communication between all scientific branches of study. Nothing short of that, carried to a far greater perfection than we have yet carried it, will really meet the needs of the situation.

Your Chairman mentioned the Committee of Civil Research. I am very much interested in that Committee, and I have had to do with it since its beginning. It is a very young mechanism, but I think it has already shown qualities which will prove invaluable in this immense task of co-ordinating all relevant knowledge. Its qualification is this. In the first place it can give no orders; nobody need be jealous of its authority because it has no authority except the authority which comes from the wisdom of its recommendations. It cannot order anybody; it cannot direct a Government Department, still less can it give directions or even

authoritative suggestions to bodies which are outside Government Departments.   And yet it affords
the opportunity of bringing together, almost in-
formally, the particular experts who can give the
best advice on a particular aspect of a particular
problem, and give that advice in the presence, and
with the help, of men who have other aspects of
the same great problem always before them.   Therefore, there is little chance of narrowness of view
interfering with the breadth of the method necessarily required for dealing with these great problems.   However, I am not going to dwell upon the
Committee of Civil Research; I only mention it because it is one of the many methods by which this
increased co-operation between workers in what are
apparently most diverse walks of life can be effected;
by which they can be brought together in focusing
their efforts upon one particular aspect of one particular problem at a time.   Only by that method,
does it seem to me, can we deal with all the matters
that come before us.

I may incidentally remark that one of the uses
to which this new mechanism of the Committee of
Civil Research has been put is in dealing with the
most obviously pressing of these scientific and
biological questions which meet us in Africa—I
mean the problem of the tsetse fly.   There are great
authorities here on that subject.   It is an appalling
reflection that the greatest of all prehistoric discoveries—the discovery of the domestic animal, or the
creation of the domestic animal—over a vast area
of Africa is rendered impossible.   You cannot use

domestic animals for the purpose of transport simply because you are conquered by this problem of the tsetse fly.   Our predecessors were wont to say that man was the crown of creation, and I do not at all deny it; but man is having a very hard fight of it with organisms which are not the crown of creation, and it is not perfectly clear to me as yet that man is getting the best of the fight.   At any rate, there are reasons, and there are aspects, of medical science, which almost indicate that at present the battle is not going in favour of the superior animal! I do not know why I embarked upon this parenthesis, because it has nothing to do with my general argument.

The point I am coming to is this.   If what we want now more than anything else, is to combine the separate forces of separate branches of science and knowledge, Societies like this are an absolutely necessary part of the machine.   Just think what an investigator—in Africa, let us say, as Africa is our main theme—has to go through.   He takes his medical degree and he goes out to a remote, outlying part of the Colonial Empire, and finds himself face to face not only with strictly medical problems, but also with the anthropological side of those problems, which cannot be absent from the thoughts of anybody who tries to deal with the native races.   He finds himself forced by his own sense of the necessity of the situation, to do research work, and at the same time finds himself very often overloaded with the routine work of turning to practical account amongst the population with which he has to deal, research work which has been already accomplished. He finds very few companions who understand either the objects for which he is working, or the methods by which he is working, or the ends for which he is working. It is of immense advantage to him, not merely that he can get the Transactions of a learned Society like this, one which deals with his subjects, enlightening him and helping him, but that he can feel he is part of the great machine which is attempting to deal in a broad spirit with all these problems. He knows that when he comes home he will find in a Society like this those who can help him in his troubles; he finds many men who will help him in his further course; he finds in the publications of this Society means which will prevent him repeating the experiments which have already been satisfactorily accomplished, and which will direct him on the lines on which research is still further to be pressed.

I cannot conceive of a greater benefit to the cause of that portion of our task in Africa which directly depends on medical science—and it is the greatest portion—than that rendered by a Society of this kind. It was started by men who were the authors and pioneers of modern Tropical Medicine, and it has been carried on by successors not unworthy even of their great fame, and I am sure I am meeting the inner sentiments and hopes of every man and woman whom I am addressing at this moment, when I wish long life, great success, and an increased sphere of usefulness to this great Society of whom I have the honour to be the guest to-night.

# 6

## On Work Done by the Civil Research Committee, and by the Department of Scientific and Industrial Research

*Speech in the House of Lords, May 12th, 1927*

I AM not going to dilate upon the subject of the labours of the Civil Research Committee, but a certain amount of publicity has already been given to the results of some of their researches which may with advantage be brought under one category. Let me just mention some of the subjects.

The first I have on my list is the tsetse fly, which, as everyone knows, is one of the most embarrassing scourges of Africa. And it is not one which merely embarrasses agriculture and destroys animal life, but is one which also destroys human life. It affects many of our Dependencies, it blasts huge areas with its unhappy curse, and it does not fall naturally under the purview of any single Department. For that reason it is exactly one of the subjects with which it is most desirable to deal and it is accordingly the subject of inquiry by the Civil Research Committee.

Another inquiry relates to the mineral content of pasture. It is a very recent discovery that pasture may have an appearance of being rich and flourishing, that it may have suffered no apparent deterioration, and yet may gradually lose its power of sustaining in healthy life the same stock which it easily has supported for a number of years.   Perhaps the expression "discovery" is not quite appropriate.   It would be more accurate to say that the importance of these mineral constituents has become a subject of study, and that it affects not merely the pastures in Scotland, but the pastures in Africa and the pastures in very many parts of the Empire.   There is one of our Colonies, the Falkland Islands, where the lack of these constituents has really produced disastrous results.   The whole subject is now under the investigation of the Civil Research Committee.

Another subject is that of native diet in Africa, and another is the Empire supply of quinine. Hitherto quinine has been almost entirely derived from certain of the Dutch Colonies.   There is no reason that we know of why that absolutely essential drug should not be cultivated elsewhere, and that is being made the subject of inquiry by the Civil Research Committee.   "The British Pharmacopœia," of which a new edition is urgently required, and which is being framed, as far as possible, upon lines suitable to the Empire, is also a subject which has come before the Civil Research Committee.   I do not want to detain your Lordships too long, and the subject I have to deal with is a big one, so that the last thing I shall mention is that of the Severn Barrage.

The Severn Barrage is rather interesting as an illustration of the value of the Civil Research Committee.   That was under the Scientific and Industrial Research Department, and they did a great deal of very valuable work upon it. It has now, however, got beyond a single Department. Other Departments are required to give their assistance and advice. It involves the Admiralty, it involves a large number of questions, geological and sociological, and it has now been handed over to the more general treatment with which the Civil Research Committee was intended to cope.

The work of the Committee of Civil Research is done by Sub-Committees which are infinitely various in their composition. This composition entirely depends upon the subject that comes under their notice, and even the imperfect enumeration which I have just given shows that the variety of subjects can hardly be exceeded by anything that is likely to arise in the future. When we go from the Severn Barrage to the tsetse fly, and the mineral content of pasture, we traverse a vast area, and that is characteristic of the work which is performed by the very elastic Committee of Civil Research.

Before I go on to my other topic, namely, the Committee of Scientific and Industrial Research— let me say, incidentally, that of course the House must not for a moment suppose that the activities of this country in the way of scientific research are exhausted either by the Committee of Industrial Research or by the Committee of Civil Research.

There is, for example, within the ambit of the Privy Council the whole immense sphere of Medical Research. Of that I mean to say nothing to-day. I say nothing, again, about the agricultural research carried on by the Agricultural Departments of England and Scotland.   But I want the country to realise that the work of the Committee of Civil Research and the Scientific and Industrial Research Department is but a portion of the Government activities devoted to the great subject of applying scientific discovery to the amelioration of the lot of mankind, and perhaps I ought to add, to the power of one set of men to destroy another, which is also a subject of Government research, unfortunately, in all countries of the world at this moment.

There are, in addition, a large number of decentralised bodies which, subject to the Advisory Committee and the Department, are carrying on, as it were, on their own.   The programmes which are allotted to them are decentralised, and they are not interfered with in the details of their labours, but they are the very backbone of all the work that is being done by the Department as a whole.   The House will see how immense is the area that they cover.

There will have to be, unless I am greatly mistaken, another decentralised body, created to deal with river pollution.   As your Lordships may be aware, this is a subject that is rapidly beginning to cause considerable anxiety to the community from many points of view—from the point of view of lovers of scenery and lovers of sport, and from the point of view of health, and the water-user.   That is a problem of great difficulty and importance, and according to my belief it will never be adequately solved without scientific investigation.

There are people who are happy enough to imagine that by reconstituting, revivifying or manipulating your local authorities, and by passing very stringent laws, the problem can be solved. But when all has been done that can be done by legislation and by re-arranging, revivifying or stimulating local author-ities, you will not satisfactorily solve the problems unless you accompany that improvement of ma-chinery and organisation with an increased knowl-edge of how you are going to deal with the effluence of factories—of the new sugar factories, for in-stance—and of sewage, without destroying those industries. If you had unlimited money and it did not matter how much it cost to purify the effluence of these factories, it could be done to-morrow, but you would destroy the industries in the process, and that is a contingency that cannot be contemplated. You have to keep your industries and you have to make the necessary scientific discoveries that will enable you, while keeping them, to purify the water from the point of view both of the water-drinker and of the fisherman. That is a biggish problem.

Before I sit down I feel disposed, merely by way of illustration, to give one or two specimens of the kind of work which has been done. The amount of money spent on research is very large and there are people wholly ignorant of what science has done, is doing and can do, who are very much inclined to say that these are impracticable suggestions, the off-spring of professors' brains, and that all that is required to maintain the industrial position of this country is to encourage the practical instincts of the ordinary Englishman, and to let him follow, like his forefathers, in the obvious path of plain, uninstructed progress. I not only disagree with that, but I believe that if that view got widely diffused among our people it would really mean the ruin of British industry. Nobody who has the smallest and most superficial acquaintance with the sort of things done in Germany, with the sort of things done in France, and in America, with the number of scientific men who are brought in to help in the solution of these problems, can possibly entertain so absurd a view of the needs of this country, and of the proper way to meet those needs.

I quite agree that when you are discussing this question with the Philistine he says: "Well, show me the financial result of your scientific research." It is quite easy to do it, but it takes a long time to do it, and some of the most important financial results cannot be simply and easily extracted from the facts.

But it is not difficult to give specimens of the kind of work which is done under the inspiration and by the help of science, which could not possibly be done in any other way. Amongst the first and greatest of the decentralised institutions is the National Physical Laboratory. Its work was originally confined to dealing with minute measurements—with standards of extreme accuracy—accuracy of certainly invisible and almost inconceivable degrees of precision. I dare say that the advocates of the old uninstructed system to whom I have alluded would say: What is the use of that? We do not live in a

world of minute measurements.  They may satisfy
the theoretical man of science, and be even desirable
from a purely speculative point of view, but for
mere practical day-to-day work they are mere over-
refinements.

What is the fact?  The fact is that so far from
ministering merely to the unnecessary refinement of
the speculative man of science, so far from satisfy-
ing a craving for complete but unnecessary accuracy,
it is on these very minute accuracies of measure-
ment that mass production is made possible.  I am
informed that if, for example, in the motor industry,
you want to have mass production it is quite obvious
there must be no time spent in fitting.  The fitting
must be automatic.  All the parts must be ready to
fit in their proper places without further manipula-
tion.  When assembled they must be put together
without difficulty.  Only on that condition can you
get mass production.  I am informed that if you
wish to do that, you must have accuracy of measure-
ment in the parts which are assembled between a
thousandth of an inch and ten-thousandths of an
inch.  I am informed that if you want to get the
parts accurate, say, to ten-thousandths of an inch,
you must be accurate up to a hundred-thousandths of
an inch, and that then, and then only, will you be
able to carry out these miraculous mass productions
which are the essential conditions of producing for
vast populations cheaply, effectually, and with no
ill-results.  I cannot imagine a more striking practical example.  I dare say there are many others far
more interesting than this, of the power of minute

measurements, but there is a practical example which even the dullest and most prosaic user of a motor-car may well take to heart.

Let me give another instance. This is the result of investigation made by another of those decentralised bodies of which I have spoken—the one which is concerned with food. The problem of the perishing of apples on their way from Australia to this country involved in one year a loss of £250,000, and the cause of the destruction of the apples in transit was a source of great anxiety and quite unexplained. The problem was laid before the Food Commission. They investigated it, and they discovered a cause which is very interesting in itself. They discovered that when you are dealing with picked apples in transit, you are not dealing with the dead, but with the living. These apples are alive, are breathing—are breathing exactly like the noble Lords whom I am addressing. They are breathing in oxygen, they are breathing out carbon-dioxide. And these apples were dying of suffocation. It was the old problem of the Black Hole of Calcutta. I consider that very interesting in itself, and not only interesting in itself, but it is going to save £250,000 a year to the apple-growers. And that is purely the result of scientific research, and could never have been discovered by any man who was not accustomed to look at these problems from the biological as well as from the ordinary everyday point of view.

I will only give one other illustration, that is, of an investigation under the chairmanship of Sir

Alfred Ewing, Head of the University of Edinburgh, and himself an engineer of the very greatest distinction. This Committee, with the help, and largely at the cost, of the railway companies, are investigating the effect of train traffic upon steel bridges. It is a problem most important to railway companies and, in a secondary sense, most important to the public at large. They have taken a great deal of trouble. They have invented some admirable instruments for testing the strain and stresses which happen when trains go over bridges, and they have arrived at a very interesting and a very important practical conclusion. I suppose I am not misrepresenting the older practice when I say that an engineer, in dealing with a bridge, is content if he knows the maximum load which that bridge would ever have to sustain. If, for instance, it is a double line, the load would be two trains; if it is a single line, it would be one train. Then, having discovered the maximum load, he adds whatever he thinks proper in the way of a large margin of safety above that which is required to sustain the load. That is a good rough and ready method, but it is extremely unscientific.

They have now, I understand, found that you must examine not merely the load the bridge carries, but the effect of the passage of the engine over the bridge. Henceforth no wise man will build a steel bridge over a railway without knowing what kind of engine is going to traverse that bridge. Formerly the idea of saying to an engineer, "Well, your bridge may be good enough for this engine, but it is not good enough for that one," would have seemed an absurd statement, but now we know that it appears to be the literal truth. Therefore when you build your bridges to suit your engines, and build your engines to suit your bridges, you will be able to get at less cost and with less material the same margin of safety. I think that interconnection, fairly obvious when stated but never thought of before, between the character of the engine which goes over the line and the stresses on the bridge which sustain the line is very interesting scientifically and mechanically, and it is going to be, I believe, very important from an industrial point of view.

I am ashamed of the length at which I have spoken, but I cannot sit down without asking your Lordships to realise the enormous value of the practically unpaid work given by these great men of science to the problems which are put before them. The members of my Council have a small honorarium, nothing that is intended to look like payment for their services, but is payment for their travelling expenses and the incidental cost of the work they do. But the work itself is done for nothing; the work itself is done for the public, and it is admirably done. I do not believe we could have got on in the degree to which we have got on, had we not the command of these great men. They really are great men. They are some of the most eminent men of science in the world and to us they devote without grudging, in a perfectly impartial spirit wholly unconnected with personal profit, direct or indirect, the whole wealth of their genius and their accomplishments.  I am glad to have an opportunity, which does not occur in the ordinary course of administrative life, of making this public statement of the great debt which, in my opinion, the whole community owes to their labours.

# 7
## On Imperial Defence*

*Remarks from the Chair after Sir Maurice Hankey's
Address on the Committee of Imperial Defence,
delivered at the London School of Economics,
March 11th, 1927*

How to treat the problem of national defence as
what it really is—a single whole—has preoccupied
many thinkers. For States whose only perils come
either from hostile armies or from hostile fleets, the
question may seem less pressing. But for us who
are amphibious, whose insular position without command of the sea would be a peril rather than a
security, whose proximity to Europe and whose Imperial responsibilities make an Army and an Air
Force absolute necessities, the question of co-
ordination becomes of most obvious importance.

For this reason I have a considerable sympathy,
not, indeed, with the suggestion that we ought to
have a Ministry of Defence, but with the aspirations underlying it; for the idea underlying it is the
idea of co-ordination. Those who desire a Ministry
of Defence desire it because they think it would give
us a degree of co-ordination which at the present
time, in their view, we only imperfectly possess. I
think there are many objections of an administrative kind to the scheme which are not germane to

*Corrected by Lord Balfour.

our subject.  There is, however, one who does immediately concern us.  I dislike a Ministry of Defence not because it forces co-ordination on us where co-ordination is not required, but because it is wholly incapable of giving us the degree of co-ordination which seems to me absolutely necessary. What a Ministry of Defence professes to do is to co-ordinate the Fighting Services.  But what, ladies and gentlemen, in these modern days are the Fighting Services?  The Fighting Services are the cutting edge of a defensive mechanism which includes every Department of State, and all the national energies which these departments control or direct. Great is the difference in this respect between modern war and the wars of even one hundred years ago.  The wars of a hundred years ago were professional wars.  The wars of to-day are national wars; not national merely in the sense of dealing with great national interests, but national in the sense of requiring every unit in the nation to bear its own share of a burden which in other times was almost wholly borne by the Army and the Navy.  Now it is surely self-evident that you cannot possibly co-ordinate all the forces of a nation if you limit your co-ordinating machinery to the three Fighting Services.  And one of the immense advantages of the Committee of Imperial Defence is that it does deliberately and explicitly include within the sphere of its considerations every department of the Government, and, in time of war, every national activity, which can be enlisted in support of the common cause.

But although this is one of the greatest services which the Committee of Imperial Defence performs, it is not the only one. It has performed, and is performing, another duty which, for sheer want of proper machinery, was never adequately attempted before. It sets itself out to foresee the kind of strain which at the outbreak of war will suddenly be imposed upon the whole social system of a modern State, and, as far as possible, to prepare beforehand the means of mitigating its effects. The danger I speak of hangs over all belligerent countries; but to us it is specially menacing. Our Empire is scattered all over the world; its separate parts are divided by vast oceans; their frontiers are of limitless length; no portions of them can be treated as the inevitable theatre of a defensive struggle; we are dependent for our very existence on the maintenance of economic conditions which are complicated, delicate, and in some respects peculiarly open to attack. If you add to those special difficulties the wider consideration that our Imperial Constitution, containing many autonomous elements, cannot, from the nature of the case, be worked with the smooth rapidity of a centralised State, it will become abundantly clear that, for us, the problems of war stretch far beyond the administrative limits of the great Fighting Services.

These are considerations which ought not to be, and I am sure will not be, forgotten by anyone who tries to estimate the advantages we have obtained from the institution of the Committee of Defence. But there is another aspect of the subject which I think deserves consideration—I mean the constitutional aspect. It is not always easy to make even the most useful addition to a historic structure like that of the British Empire without inflicting some injury on its more ancient parts. This danger the Committee of Imperial Defence has, I think, completely avoided. It provides (as we have seen) a continuing instrument of organised consultation between experts within and without the Government Departments, the Ministers responsible to the British Parliament, and, when they desire it, the Ministers responsible to the Dominion Parliaments also. It therefore touches our national and imperial life at innumerable points. But nowhere, and under no conditions, can it modify or limit parliamentary control or ministerial responsibility; and though it may find itself (if circumstances require) in closest relations with any or every Department of State, yet this cannot engender either friction or jealousy. The Committee is not a super-Department; it has no executive responsibilities; it gives no orders; it only gives advice; and in framing that advice the representatives of all the Departments concerned are sure to take their share. It thus supplies a machinery which is not only cheap, efficient, and infinitely flexible; but one which can give help to all Governments whatever their political complexion, though it cannot shelter any Minister or any Government from the parliamentary consequences of their own bad luck or bad management.

# SECTION V
# ZIONISM

I

## On Great Britain and Zionism

*Speech at the Albert Hall at a Demonstration
organised by the English Zionist Federation, to
thank the British Government for the decision
to incorporate the Balfour Declaration for a
Jewish National Home in the Treaty of Peace
with Turkey, July 12th, 1920*

For long I have been a convinced Zionist, and it
is in that character that I come before you to-day,
though in my most sanguine moments I never fore-
saw, I never even conceived, the possibility that the
great work of Palestinian reconstruction would happen so soon, or that indeed it was likely to happen in
my own lifetime. This is one of the great and un-
expected results of the world struggle which has
just come to an end—even if, indeed, we dare to say
that it has yet completely come to an end. Of
infinite evils that struggle has been the parent, but
if among its results we can count the re-establish-
ment in their ancient home of the Jewish people, at
all events we can put to its credit one great result
which under other circumstances, so far as we can
see, could never have occurred at so early a date.
Who would have thought five or six years ago
that a speaker in the Albert Hall would be able

to recount as an accomplished fact that the Great Powers of the world had elected to accept the Declaration to which Lord Rothschild has referred, had consented to give a Mandate to the country which at all events is in the forefront among those who desire to see this policy brought to a successful issue, and that they would already have seen appointed as the High Commissioner of Palestine a man who so admirably joins the double qualifications which Lord Rothschild has so felicitously expressed?  These are happy results, these are results on which we may all congratulate ourselves.

Let us not forget in our feelings of legitimate triumph all the difficulties which still lie before us. Those difficulties I have no hesitation in dwelling upon, because I know that you will overcome them; yet it is worth while to enumerate some of them, not to discourage you, but to raise your courage and your resolution even to a higher pitch than it has already reached.  Among these difficulties I am not sure that I do not rate highest, or at all events first, the inevitable difficulty of dealing with the Arab question as it presents itself within the limits of Palestine.  It will require tact, it will require judgment, it will require above all sympathetic goodwill on the part both of Jew and of Arab.

So far as the Arabs are concerned—a great, an interesting, and an attractive race—I hope they will remember that while this assembly and all Jews that it represents through the world desire under the ægis of Great Britain to establish this home for the Jewish people, the Great Powers, and among all the Great Powers most especially Great Britain, has freed them, the Arab race, from the tyranny of their brutal conqueror, who had kept them under his heel for these many centuries. I hope they will remember it is we who have established the independent Arab sovereignty of the Hejaz. I hope they will remember that it is we who desire in Mesopotamia to prepare the way for the future of a self-governing, autonomous Arab State, and I hope that, remembering all that, they will not grudge that small notch—for it is no more geographically, whatever it may be historically—that small notch in what are now Arab territories, being given to the people who for all these hundreds of years have been separated from it—but surely have a title to develop on their own lines in the land of their forefathers, which ought to appeal to the sympathy of the Arab people as it, I am convinced, appeals to the great mass of my own Christian fellow-countrymen. That is the first difficulty. That can be got over and will be got over, by mutual goodwill.

The second difficulty, on which I shall only say a word, arises from the fact that the critics of this movement shelter themselves behind the principle of self-determination, and say that, if you apply that principle logically and honestly, it is to the majority of the existing population of Palestine that the future destinies of Palestine should be committed. There is a technical ingenuity in that plea, and on technical grounds I neither can nor desire to provide the answer; but looking back upon the history of the world, upon the history more particularly of

all the most civilised portions of the world, I say
that the case of Jewry in all countries is absolutely
exceptional, falls outside all the ordinary rules and
maxims, cannot be contained in a formula or explained in a sentence.  The deep underlying principle
of self-determination really points to a Zionist
policy, however little in its strict technical inter-
pretation it may seem to favour it.  I am convinced
that none but pedants, or people who are prejudiced
by religious or racial bigotry, would deny for one
instant that the case of the Jews is absolutely exceptional, and must be treated by exceptional methods.

The third difficulty is of a wholly different order
of magnitude and character—it is the physical
difficulty.  Palestine, great as is the place which
it occupies in the history of the world, is but a
small and petty country looked at as a geographical
unit; and men ask themselves how in these narrow
limits—to be traversed easily in an automobile in
an easy day's journey from Dan to Beersheba—it
can be made physically adequate to be the home for
the self-development of the Jewish people.

The problem presents difficulties, at present no
impossibilities.  It presents difficulties which I myself should regard as overwhelming were we dealing
with another people and with different conditions.
But what are the requisites of such development in
Palestine as may accommodate an important section
of the great race that I am addressing?  What are
the two necessities?  One is skill, knowledge, per-
severance, enterprise; the other is capital; and I am
perfectly convinced that when you are talking of the

Jews you will find no want of any one of these requisites.  Of skill, of knowledge, of all that the most
modern methods can teach in the way of engineer-
ing or of agriculture, the Jewish race, who have
themselves contributed to the result, can easily make
themselves the master.  And when I consider capital
I am not thinking of the great millionaires, of the
men of vast wealth belonging to the Jewish race.
I doubt not that they will do their duty; but it is not
of them I am thinking—I am thinking of the innumerable Jews in the poorest circumstances, for I
have heard authentic tales of the manner in which,
out of their poverty, they are prepared to contribute
to the success of this enterprise.

The fourth and the last difficulty on which I
want to speak is perhaps in some respects the greatest of all.  This movement cannot be carried out
except by idealists.  No man who is incapable of
idealism is capable either of understanding the Zionist Movement or effectually contributing to its
consummation; but idealism, though a necessary
element in every great and fruitful policy, has its
inevitable dangers itself.  Your cynic, your man of
narrow and selfish views does nothing; your idealist
does much.  But he does not always do the right
thing, and the very qualities which make a man
sacrifice all that he has for an idea very often blind
him to that cool and calm judgment without which
great ideas cannot be brought to a true and successful fruition.

I speak as a man who is not a Jew, and who
necessarily, therefore, looks at the Jewish question

from outside; but I should say that perhaps the danger which besets the Jewish race is not that they lack idealism, not that they are reluctant to sacrifice everything, even life itself, to see that ideal carried into effect, but that they are carried away by the vehemence of their passions, the depth and strength of their convictions, and they are unwilling to do that without which, believe me, this and any other great movement must necessarily fail—they are unwilling to give that whole-hearted trust and confidence in their chosen leaders which, believe me, is necessary. You are drawn from every nation under heaven; you come to London or any other great centre with ideas absorbed from the populations wherein you have sojourned. You come, therefore, with many different mentalities—to use the familiar phrase. You come perhaps with many different theories as to the method by which your common objects may be carried out. There is no harm in that; it only becomes dangerous when these different sections insist not merely that the object should be carried out, but that it should be carried out precisely in the fashion which commends itself to them. Beware of that danger. I am not sure it is not the greatest danger which may beset you in the future.

And now, ladies and gentlemen, I have done with the gloomy task of enumerating difficulties, and I have only one more word to say. We are embarked on a great adventure, and I say "we" advisedly, and by "we" I mean on the one side the Jewish people, and I mean, on the other side, the Mandatory Power

of Palestine. We are partners in this great enterprise. If we fail you, you cannot succeed. If you
fail us, you cannot succeed. But I feel assured that
we shall not fail you and that you will not fail us;
and if I am right, as I am sure I am, in this prophecy of hope and confidence, then surely we may look
forward with a happy gaze to a future in which
Palestine will indeed, and in the fullest measure and
degree of success, be made a home for the Jewish
people.

## 2

ON THE MANDATE FOR PALESTINE

*Speech in the House of Lords, June 21st, 1922*

[NOTE.—Lord Islington had given notice to move "That the Mandate for Palestine in its present form is inacceptable to this House, because it directly violates the pledges made by His Majesty's Government to the people of Palestine in the Declaration of October, 1915, and again in the Declaration of November, 1918, and is, at present framed, opposed to the sentiments and wishes of the great majority of the people of Palestine; that therefore its acceptance by the Council of the League of Nations should be postponed until such modifications have therein been effected as will comply with the pledges given by His Majesty's Government."]

As I understood the noble Lord [Lord Islington], he thinks, in the first place, that the Mandate for Palestine is inconsistent with the policy of the Powers who invented the mandatory system, and who are now carrying it into effect. That is his first charge. His second charge is that we are inflicting considerable material and political injustice upon the Arab population of Palestine. His third charge is that we have done a great injustice to the Arab race as a whole.

I should like to traverse all those statements.
Let me take them in the order in which I have
named them. I think it must have occurred to my
noble friend, when he was giving us an account of
the transactions during the War and up to the end
of the negotiation of the Treaty of Versailles, that
it was rather paradoxical to maintain that the people
who invented the mandatory system did not know
what it meant. The mandatory system always contemplated the Mandate for Palestine on the general
lines of the Declaration of November, 1917. It was
not sprung upon the League of Nations, and it was
not sprung upon the Powers that met together in
Paris to deal with the peace negotiations before the
League of Nations came into existence. It was a
settled policy among the Allied and Associated
Powers before the Armistice. It was accepted in
America, it was accepted in this country, it was published all over the world, and, if ever there was a
Declaration which had behind it a general consensus
of opinion, I believe it was the Declaration of
November, 1917.

Your Lordships may, perhaps, have in mind that
President Wilson, whose declarations were so intimately connected with the whole policy of the Mandates, was most strongly in favour of the policy
embodied in the existing Mandate, that it was
pressed upon him by the population of the United
States, that it was fully accepted by him, and that he
came to Paris to carry out, so far as the Government
was concerned, the very principles embodied in these
Mandates.

As for this country, I happen to be the mouthpiece of my colleagues in making the Declaration of November, 1917. I do not know why we have waited—I do not know why your Lordships' House has waited—until 1922 to attack a policy which was initiated in 1917 or before, which was plainly before the world and was dealt with in detail in 1919 in Paris, and is now being carried out by the Allied and Associated Powers and by the League of Nations.

Therefore, when my noble friend tries to maintain the paradox that the Powers who adopted the mandatory system, the Powers who laid down the lines on which that system was to be carried out, who have embodied it in the League of Nations, and have set going Governments in different parts of the world, who are at this moment carrying out the mandatory system, are so ignorant that they do not know their own child, and are violating all their principles when they establish the policy of a Jewish Home in Palestine, I think he is not only somewhat belated in his criticism, but is asking us to accept a proposition which, as men of common sense, we should certainly repudiate. I will therefore leave what I may call the legal or juridical aspect of the criticism of my noble friend, which I think he will admit is essentially paradoxical, and will come to his more particular charges.

Those particular charges were, in the first place, that it was impossible to establish a Jewish Home in Palestine without giving to the Jewish organisations political powers over the Arab races with which they should not be entrusted, and which, even if they exercised them well, were not powers that should be given under a British Mandate to one race over another. But I think my noble friend gave no evidence of the truth of these charges. He told us that it was quite obvious that some kind of Jewish domination over the Arabs was an essential consequence of the attempt to establish a Jewish Home. It is no necessary consequence, and it is surely a very poor compliment to the British Government, to a Governor of Palestine appointed by the British Government, to the Mandates Commission under the League of Nations, whose business it will be to see that the spirit of the Mandate as well as the letter is carried out, and beyond them to the Council of the League of Nations, to suppose that all these bodies will so violate every pledge that they have ever given, and every principle to which they have ever subscribed, as to use the power given to them by the Peace Treaty to enable one section of the community in Palestine to oppress and dominate any other.

I cannot imagine any political interests exercised under greater safeguards than the political interests of the Arab population of Palestine. Every act of the Government will be jealously watched. The Zionist organisation has no attribution of political powers. If it uses or usurps political powers it is an act of usurpation. Is that conceivable or possible under the lynx eyes of critics like my noble friend, or of the Mandates Commission, whose business it will be to see that the Mandate is carried out, or of a British Governor-General nourished and brought up under the traditions of British equality and British good government, and, finally, behind all those safe-guards, with the safe-guard of free Parliamentary criticism in this House and in the other House? These are fantastic fears. They are fears that need perturb no sober and impartial critic of contemporary events, and whatever else may happen in Palestine, I am very confident that under British Government no form of tyranny, racial or religious, will ever be permitted.

Now, I go from that broad charge of putting the Arab population under the domination of the Zionist Organisation, and I come to the more detailed attacks made by my noble friend. He criticised the whole system of immigration. I do not know why he did that. No human being supposes that Palestine is an over-populated country. It is, I believe, an under-populated country at the moment at which I speak, before all the economic developments to which I look forward have had time to take place, and if the hopes that I entertain are not widely disappointed, the power of Palestine to maintain a population far greater than she had or could ever have under Turkish rule, will be easily attained in consequence of the material well-being which under Turkish rule was wholly impossible.

The hopes that I have just expressed with regard to the growth of population in Palestine of course are necessarily based upon the amount of capital expenditure you can give to that country, upon the character of the population who are going to make use of the machinery provided by that capital expenditure, and upon the character of the Government under which all these operations will be carried out.  Now, I ask my noble friend, who takes up the cause of the Arabs, and who seems to think that their material well-being is going to be diminished under the new system, how he thinks that the existing population of Palestine is going to be effective unless and until you get capitalists to invest their money in developing the resources of this small country—small in area, though great in memories —which, according to all the information we possess, might carry a population far bigger than that which it now supports.  It can only do so, I believe, if you can draw upon the enthusiasm of the Jewish Communities throughout the world.  As soon as this Mandate question is finally settled, they will, I believe, come forward and freely help in the development of a Jewish Home.

That is not going to be a great speculative investment; that is not going to bring millions into the pockets of international finance; that is not going to prove wildly exciting upon the Stock Exchange of London or New York; that is going to be carried out as much, indeed far more, in order to carry out these great idealist designs than to earn dividends or to make fortunes.

I would like to ask my noble friend whether even from the most material point of view, it is not in the interests of the Arab population itself to encourage this great project of the Jewish Home.  My noble friend committed himself to the statement that Jews and Arabs up to the present time had enjoyed the same privileges. So they have—the privilege of being under Turkish rule. That privilege was impartially extended to every section of the population, and with the results which has not uncommonly followed the enjoyment of the same privileges, in other parts of the world.

That state of things has happily come to an end. But if the populations who were trampled under the heel of the Turk until the end of the war are really to gain all the benefits that they might, it can only be by the introduction of the most modern methods, fed by streams of capital from all parts of the world, and that can only be provided, so far as I can see, by carrying out this great scheme which the vast majority of the Jews—not all, I quite agree, and very often, perhaps, commonly not the wealthiest—the great mass of the Jews in East and West and North and South believe to be a great step forward in the alleviation of the lot which their race has had too long to bear. I do not think I need dwell upon this imaginary wrong which the Jewish Home is going to inflict upon the local Arabs.

My noble friend told us in his speech, and I believe him absolutely, that he has no prejudice against the Jews. I think I may say that I have no prejudice in their favour. But their position and their history, their connection with world religion and with world politics, is absolutely unique. There is no parallel to it, there is nothing approaching to a parallel to it, in any other branch of human history. Here you have a small race originally inhabiting a small country of about the size of Wales or Belgium, at no time in its history wielding anything that can be described as material power, sometimes crushed in between great Oriental monarchies, its inhabitants deported, then scattered, then driven out of the country altogether into every part of the world, and yet maintaining a continuity of religious and racial traditions to which we have no parallel elsewhere.

That, itself, is sufficiently remarkable, but consider how they have been treated during long centuries, during centuries which in some parts of the world extend to the minute and the hour in which I am speaking. Consider how they have been subjected to tyranny and persecution; consider whether the whole culture of Europe, the whole religious organisation of Europe, has not from time to time proved itself guilty of great crimes against this race. I quite understand that some members of the race may have given, doubtless did give, occasion for much ill-will. I do not know how it could be otherwise, treated as they were; but, if you are going to lay stress on that, do not forget what part they have played in the intellectual, the artistic, the philosophic and scientific development of the world. I say nothing of the economic side of their energies, for on that Christian attention has always been concentrated.

I ask your Lordships to consider the other side of their activities. Nobody will deny that they have at least—and I am putting it more moderately than I could do—rowed all their weight in the boat of scientific, intellectual and artistic progress, and they are doing so to this day. You will find them in every University, in every centre of learning; and at the very moment when they were being persecuted, when some of them, at all events, were being persecuted by the Church, their philosophers were developing thoughts which the great doctors of the Church embodied in their religious system. As it was in the Middle Ages, as it was in earlier times, so it is now. And yet, is there anyone here who feels content with the position of the Jews? They have been able, by this extraordinary tenacity of their race, to maintain this continuity, and they have maintained it without having any Jewish Home.

What has been the result? The result has been that they have been described as parasites on every civilisation in whose affairs they have mixed themselves—very useful parasites at times, I venture to say. But however that may be, do not your Lordships think that if Christendon, not oblivious of all the wrong it has done, can without injury to others give a chance to this race of showing whether it can organise a culture in a Home where it will be secured from oppression, that it is not well to say, if we can do it, that we will do it? And should we not be doing something material to wash out an ancient stain upon our own civilisation, if we absorb the Jewish race in friendly and effective fashion in those countries in which they are the citizens? We should then have given them what every other nation has, some place, some local habitation, where they can develop the culture and the traditions which are peculiarly their own.

I therefore frankly admit that I have been, in so far as I have had anything to do with this policy, moved by considerations which were not touched upon by my noble friend in the course of his speech. I have endeavoured, and I hope not unsuccessfully, to defend this scheme of the Palestine Mandate from the most material economic view, and from that point of view it is capable of defence. I have endeavoured to defend it from the point of view of the existing population, and I have shown that their prosperity also is intimately bound up with the success of Zionism. But having endeavoured to the best of my ability to maintain those two propositions, I should, indeed, give an inadequate view to your Lordships of my opinions if I sat down without insisting to the utmost of my ability, that, beyond and above all this, there is this great ideal at which those who think with me are aiming and which, I believe, it is within their power to reach.

It may fail: I do not deny that this is an adventure. Are we never to have adventures? Are we never to try new experiments? I hope your Lordships will never sink to that unimaginative depth, and that experiment and adventure will be justified if there is any case or cause for their justification. Surely, it is in order that we may send a message to every land where the Jewish race has been scattered, a message which will tell them that Christendom is not oblivious of their faith, is not unmindful of the service they have rendered to the great religions of the world, and that we desire to the best of our ability to give them opportunity of developing, in peace and quietness under British rule, those great gifts which hitherto they have been compelled to bring to fruition in countries which know not their language, and belong not to their race?

That is the ideal which I desire to see accomplished, that is the aim which lay at the root of the policy I am trying to defend; and though it be defensible indeed on every ground, that is the ground which chiefly moves me.

# 3

## THE OPENING OF THE HEBREW UNIVERSITY

### *Jerusalem, April, 1925*

ALLOW me to thank you in the first place for the kind reception that you have just given me. I would that I could speak to you in Hebrew, but you will have to be content with the language most familiar to me, and, I hope, not wholly unfamiliar to many of those whom I have the great honour of addressing.

What is it that has brought together this vast concourse drawn from every quarter of the world, often speaking as their mother tongue languages far separated in human speech, and all gathered here as one, a great and unique historic occasion in a land in which historic associations crowd on the memory at every step you take from north to south or east to west?

It is not the magnificence of the view which is stretched before you. It is the consciousness that this occasion marks a great epoch in the history of a people who have made this little land of Palestine a seed ground of great religion, and whose intellectual and moral destiny is again, from a national point of view, reviving, and who will look back to this day which we are celebrating as one of the great milestones in its future career.

I was a few minutes ago reminded by one friend that from where you are sitting you can see the very spot where the children of Israel first entered the Promised Land. I mentioned this to another friend, and he pointed out to me in his turn that it was from this hill, this Mount Scopus, that the Roman destroyer of Jerusalem conducted the siege which brought to an end that great chapter of the Jewish people. Could there be a more historic spot? From this hill you can see the beginning, from this you can see the end, or what appeared to be the end, of the Jewish community, and of the connection of the Jewish community with the land which they had made illustrious.

Well, a new epoch has begun. A great cultural effort within Palestine which came to an end many hundreds of years ago is going to be resumed in the ancient home of the people. It is not that I would suggest for a moment that Jewish culture in the interval between the destruction of Jerusalem and the expulsion of the Turk, that during that long period, Jewish culture had ceased. Far from it. It has been uninterrupted, but it has been scattered, it has not been the culture of the Jewish people living within the traditional limits of the country which they have rendered so famous. It was the separate effort of separate communities, separate individuals, separate men of science, separate theologians, separate philosophers, scattered over the habitable globe. They have borne their share in the progress of civilisation.

I think it is a profound mistake to suppose that

men of Jewish birth have not borne their share, their full share, their very full share, in the progress of knowledge, in the growth of human civilisation the world over. They have done so, as it were, however united in consciousness, still scattered in fact and unable to concentrate—as I hope they now will concentrate—their peculiar national genius (and every nation has its national genius) in the common task in which they have indeed aided in the past, and in which, I confidently hope, they will in the future be able to give aid ever more important. From these peculiar circumstances we are now engaged in adapting Western methods and a Western form of university, to an Asiatic site and to an education which is to be carried on in an Eastern language. That is a new experiment. It has never been tried before under any circumstances parallel at all to those in which I speak to you. Ladies and gentlemen, unless I have misunderstood the signs of the times, unless I have profoundly mistaken the genius of the Jewish people, the experiment is predestined to an inevitable success. Not only men of Jewish birth but others who share the common civilisation of the world, will have reason to congratulate themselves.

Because I speak in these tones of sanguine confidence do not for a moment suppose that I underrate the difficulties which will unquestionably meet both Dr. Weizmann, Sir Herbert Samuel, and His Excellency's successor, in the task that is before them. Do not suppose I underrate the difficulties which must necessarily beset every great enterprise,

and will certainly beset the great enterprise in
which you are all feeling a common interest. I am
not going into details of the practical difficulties
with which the founders and the guides of this University will have to deal. One which would actually
strike every person facing this problem is the
problem of language. It is true that Hebrew has
never been a dead language, but it has not been a
language, until recently, adapted to the many
phases of a modern development. It is a great
language—I say so with boldness, though I do not
know any Hebrew, and I say so for this reason, that
all the English-speaking people have been brought
up on a translation into English of the Hebrew
Scripture, and that translation is one of the great
literary treasures of all who speak the English
tongue. It matters not what their creed may be
or what the historic value of the Hebrew Bible may
be, if they know anything of the great language
of which they are heirs, they will all tell you without exception that the translation of the Hebrew
Scriptures into English has had a profound literary
effect upon the whole development of what I am
not prepared to say is inferior to any language in
any age, in its literary output.

If the translation from the Hebrew has had that
profound literary effect upon the English language,
surely I am justified in saying that the language
from which the translation was made must, like all
languages from which a translation is made, be
superior to that translation to which it has given
birth. Clearly, therefore, Jewish people have been,

and are, heirs of a great instrument of literary inspiration, an instrument capable of dealing with
all the highest aspects of literary and imaginative
literature. But does it follow from that that
Hebrew is fitted for modern uses? There is a
great difference between Isaiah and micro-biology.
Is the poetry and imagery of the language of
Isaiah fitted to deal with all the laboratory work that
is going to render this spot illustrious? I should
have anticipated that a very doubtful answer could
be given to that question were it not that competent
authorities assure me that by the genius, largely, I
am told, of one man, Hebrew has been developed and
has been placed upon lines of development, which
make it as flexible, as rich, and as capable of adap-
tion to every new use, to every growth in the realm
of knowledge, as every other language in which
human thought can be expressed, and therefore that
difficulty at least has been happily and adequately
surmounted. Another difficulty which I have been
somewhat afraid of—no, I do not think I even was
afraid, but some people were afraid of it: it was the
difficulty that there would not be adequate teachers
to deal with the whole circuit, the growing and
spreading circuit, of human knowledge. Well, I
think that if those who entertain that particular
form of scepticism will only look for what men of
Hebrew birth have done and are doing in the very
realm of work to which your University is to be
specially devoted, all their fears will melt away, and
they will experience the confidence which most of
you, and I, certainly share in the future.

In recent years (what I am going to say is merely an illustration of the competence of men of Hebrew birth in their special scientific lines), in the last few years there have been three theories all relating to different branches of science, three theories which have attracted the attention even of the unscientific. I have no doubt that they have promoted a great deal of unintelligible small talk; nevertheless they have produced an enormous impression in all parts of the world among all celebrated societies. One of these is the philosophic theory known generally as the theory of creative evolution, and the author of that is my friend Mr. Bergson, a great philosopher and a Jew. Another theory much talked of, or rather another group of theories, constitute what is called the new psychology. The author of that is my friend, also a Jew. The third theory, the most comprehensive, the most original, and the most important of all, is the theory of relativity. That, as we know, is largely the work of Mr. Einstein, a mathematical scientific genius of the first order, who is also a Jew.

I do not mean to suggest even to this audience that all the great scientific work of the world has been and is being done, or is going to be done, by men of Jewish birth. It certainly is not, but it is worth notice by those who look with doubt and scepticism on the ideal of a Jewish University in Palestine devoted to scientific research, what an important place at the present moment with regard to the immediate problems which are interesting in-

telligent mankind the Jewish race has made and is
making in our day.

There has been a good deal of criticism upon
recent developments in this country from the Arab
point of view, and it has been said that in a Hebrew
University the Arabs can play little part, that from
a Hebrew University the Arab race can derive but
little advantage. There is no doubt that the University must be a Hebrew University. There is no
doubt that the language of the University must be
Hebrew, but it is a profound mistake to suppose that
on that account the Arab population in this country
cannot draw the measure of advantage which a University is capable of giving to those whom it serves.
I hope Arabs will remember that in the darkest days
of the Dark Ages, when Western civilisation appeared almost extinct, smothered under barbaric
influences, that it was the Jews and Arabs in combination, working together, who greatly aided the first
sparks of light which illuminated the gloomy period.
If in the tenth century, for example, Jews and Arabs
could work together for the illumination of Europe,
cannot Jews and Arabs work together now in co-
operation with Europe, and make this not merely a
great Palestinian University but a Palestinian University from which all sections of the population of
Palestine may draw intellectual and spiritual advantage?

Ladies and gentlemen, you have won this land
which is the seed-ground of great religions. Its
immortal claim to the gratitude of mankind largely

rests upon that, but it has had, we all know, the effect of making this little country the scene of endless disputes, endless differences, endles controversies and troubles. To look at the spires and domes, the endless ecclesiastical monuments in Jerusalem, is an almost startling reminder of how far religious differences can divide mankind. Therefore again I say the difficulty is one which needs consideration. Yet if people would only look sufficiently deeply they would find that there are fundamental principles, fundamental inspirations in which they all agree. Those differences I know well are inevitable. We ought to minimise them, but we cannot deny that they exist, and we cannot hope that they will not be lasting. But the great happiness of the endeavour on which we are all engaged at this moment is that it does not divide: the endeavour to found a new University on worthy lines ought not to be interfered with by these ancient sources of differences which have so unhappily divided mankind. Science at least is outside these sectarian differences. It changes, it moves in these days of ours, it moves with extreme rapidity, but at any one moment at any period in the development of knowledge you will find that, broadly speaking, all competent men are agreed, not as to what is the ultimate truth but what is at the moment the best truth which you can arrive at, and from that progress starts and forms a new base for a new advancement.

The learning of the modern University is not a cause of separation and difference between men. It is a bond of union. Learning is a bond which unites

all men by means of adequate instruction in all parts
of the world. It affords a common base of thought
which provides common hopes for the future. It
supplies a common interest, and every student in
every University knows that he has among his
colleagues not only those working around him, but
men from distant lands on the other side of the
globe, coping with the same problems, dealing with
the same difficulties, solving the same enigmas.

The discoverer in the most abstract branches of
science is serving not merely the spiritual but the
material interests of the human race in ways of
which he himself never dreams. Each development
will be pursued later by other men, used by other
workers in the same fields, and in the end will benefit
men who know nothing of science, will benefit those
to whom science seems an almost contemptible and
unpractical pursuit. The world nevertheless would
never share in the progress of civilisation were it
not for the practical application of theoretical knowledge to the needs of human kind. If we keep these
two ideas in view—the idea of knowledge for its
own sake and the idea of knowledge as the minister
of human material well-being—could you pursue a
better course than that which Dr. Weizmann and
his colleagues have pursued, namely, to select as the
first branch of work on which they are going to
throw their scientific efforts, these rapidly advanc-
ing spheres of knowledge which touch the health
of man, the prosperity of the agriculural industries
by which man ultimately lives? I believe that under
their auspices you will find that this University car-

ries out effectually the double task it is entrusted with, the task in the first place of augmenting human knowledge irrespective of the use to which the knowledge is to be applied; and, secondly, the practical side which turns to account day by day the discoveries which the men of genius, the men of ideal genius, are developing elsewhere.

I am confident that that happy result is one to which we may confidently look forward, for we live in an age of unequalled rapidity in scientific discovery. When I was born the very names of the sciences which you will find mentioned in that pamphlet and those to which the University is going to devote its infant energies, were unknown and unused.

It is not too much to say that in the course of one man's life our whole outlook upon nature has been fundamentally altered. That is the very moment at which I should desire a University based on research to come into being; that is the happy moment when it may take its share in this great harvest of increasing knowledge which is being garnered in every part of the world. It is because I am confident that in that great task the University of Jerusalem is going to play no small or ignoble part, but is going to be, indeed is, animated by ideals as high as those of any University, that it will be staffed and composed of men not inferior to men in any part of the world in their scientific capacity. It is for those reasons that in supreme confidence in its future I declare the Hebrew University to be opened.

SECTION VI
# INTERNATIONAL AFFAIRS

# I

## ON ANGLO-AMERICAN FRIENDSHIP*

*Speech at the Pilgrims' Dinner, Fourth of July,*
1917

ON this anniversary in every part of the world American citizens meet together and renew, as it were, their vows of devotion to the great ideals which have animated them. All the world admires, all the world sympathises with the vast work of the great American Republic. All the world looks back upon the one hundred and forty-one years which have elapsed since the Declaration of Independence, and sees in that one hundred and forty-one years an expansion in the way of population, in the way of wealth and of power, material and spiritual, which is unexampled in that period in the history of the world.

We of the British race, who do not fall short of the rest of the world in our admiration of this mighty work, look at it in some respects in a different way, and must look at it in a different way from that of other people. From one point of view we have surely a right to look at it with a special satisfaction, a satisfaction born of the fact that, after

*Another aspect of this subject is dealt with in No. 1 of Section VII on Golf.

all, the thirteen colonies were British colonies; that the thirteen colonies, in spite of small controversies, grew up, broadly speaking, under the protection of England; that it was our wars, the English wars with Spain in the sixteenth century, with Holland in the seventeenth century, and with France in the eighteenth century, which gave that security from external European attack which enabled those thir- teen colonies to develop into the nucleus of the great community of which they were the origin.

We British may also surely, without undue vanity, pride ourselves on the fact that the men who founded the great American Republic, the men whose genius contrived its constitution, their forefathers, who, struggling in the wilderness, gradually devel- oped the basis of all that has happened since, were men speaking the English language, obeying and be- lieving in English laws, and nourished upon English literature. Although we may say that the origi- nality and power and endurance were theirs, they were men of our own race, born of the same stock, and to that extent at least we may feel that we have some small but not insignificant part in the great development which the world owes to their genius, courage, and love of liberty.

In that sense we may look with peculiar pride and satisfaction upon this great anniversary. There is, of course, another side to the question. The 4th of July is the anniversary of the separation, the final political separation—not, thank God, the final separation in sentiment, in emotion, or in ideal— but the final political separation between the thirteen colonies and the Mother Country. We of the Mother Country cannot look back on that event as representing one of our successes. No doubt there was something to be said, though perhaps it is not often said, for those on this side of the Atlantic who fought for unity, who desired to preserve the unity of the Empire. Unity is a cause for which the American people have sacrificed rivers of blood and infinite treasure.

I am not going into ancient history, but the mistake we made, an almost inevitable mistake at that particular period of the development of the history of the world, was in supposing that unity was possible so long as one part of the Empire which you tried to unite, speaking the same language, having the same traditions and laws, having the same love of liberty and the same ideals, would consent to remain a part of the Empire, except on absolutely equal terms. That was a profound mistake, a mistake which produced a great schism and produced all the collateral, though I am glad to think subordinate, evils which followed on that great schism.

All I can say in excuse for my forefathers is that, utterly defective as the Colonial policy of Great Britain in the middle of the eighteenth century undoubtedly was, it was far better than the Colonial policy of any other country. Imperfectly as we conceived the kind of relations that might, or could, bind the Colonies to their Mother Country, thoroughly as we misconceived them, we misconceived them less than most of our neighbours.

I went on Monday last to the ceremonial at

Westminster Abbey in which the fiftieth anniversary of the Constitution of Canada was celebrated. There is a great difference between fifty years and one hundred and forty-one years. It took us a long time to learn the lesson that if you want to make an Empire of different widely separated communities of the British race you must do it on terms of absolute equality. We have learnt the lesson and in our own way we are now carrying out as great, as momentous, and even a more difficult task than fell to the great and illustrious framers of the American Constitution. We are endeavouring to carry out by slow degrees an Imperial Constitution which shall combine this absolute equality of different communities with the machinery for the perpetual attainment of common imperial ends.

But that great experiment was begun in its fullness only fifty years ago, within my lifetime. It will take the lifetime of many generations of statesmen all over the world in this great and scattered Empire to bring it to a full and successful fruition.

It is impossible not to speculate as to how many ills would have been spared if in 1776 those who preceded us could have foreseen the future and understood wherein the true path of political wisdom lay. Many people have plunged in endless speculations as to what would have happened if there had been no violent division between the two great sections of our people. I do not follow them in those speculations. No man can do so. No man can say what would have happened if a country which has now one hundred millions of population, with infinite resources and admirable organisation, had never formally been separated from these small islands.   But this at all events would have happened. The separation, if and when it had occurred, would have been a friendly separation. There would never have been a memory of the smallest kind dividing the feelings of those, every one of whose emotions moved in the same key to be directed towards the same end.   That would have been a great gain.   It is a loss to us in this country.   I almost venture to say it might have been in some respects a loss to those of you, the great mass of my audience, who own a different allegiance.   It would have been an infinite gain if there had been no memory in either of two nations which pointed to sharp divisions, to battles lost and won, with all the evils of war, with all the evils of defeat, with all the evils, almost as great, of victory, if any sting or soreness remained behind.

If I rightly read the signs of the times, a truer and a more charitable perspective is now recognised and felt by all the heirs of these sad and ancient glories.   Heaven knows I do not grudge the glories of Washington and his brother soldiers.   I do not drop tears over the British defeat which ended in the triumphant establishment of the American Republic. I do not express any regrets on that subject. My only regrets are that the memories of it should carry with them the smallest trace of bitterness on our side.   I do not know why there should be.   I think it may properly carry memories of triumph on your side, but it should be a triumph seen in its true perspective, in such a way that it does not interfere with the continuity of history in the development of free institutions, with the consciousness of common kinship and common ideals, and the considerations which ought to bind us together, and which have bound us together, and which day by day and year by year, generation by generation, and century by century, are going to bind us still closer together in the future.

Therefore it is that I rejoice to find myself joining with my American friends in celebrating this great anniversary. Hitherto, from the necessities of history, battles that have been waged on American soil have been battles waged between people of the same speech and of the same traditions. In the future the ideas which, even in the moment of struggle were always fundamentally and essentially the same, find a sphere of action outside even the ample limits of the United States, and bind us together in a world task. That is the great thought. We are not brought together in this colossal struggle; we are not working together at this identical moment—this great and unsurpassed moment in the history of the world—aiming at narrow or selfish objects; or bound together partly by the antiquated traditions. We are working together in all the freedom of great hopes and with great ideals. Those hopes and those ideals we have not learnt from each other. We have them in common from a common history and from a common ancestry. We have not learnt freedom from you, nor you from us. We both spring from the same root. We both cultivate the same great aims.  We both have the same hopes as regards the future of Western civilisation, and now we find ourselves united in this great struggle against a Power which, if it be allowed to prevail, is going to destroy the very roots of that Western civilisation from which we all draw our strength.  We are bound together in that.

Are we not bound together for ever?  Will not our descendants, when they come to look back upon this unique episode in the history of the world, say that among the incalculable circumstances which it produces, the most beneficent and the most permanent is, perhaps, that we are brought together and united for one common purpose in one common understanding—the two great branches of the English-speaking race?

That is the theme which I have endeavoured to develop to-night.  It is a theme which absorbs my thoughts day and night.  It is a theme which moves me more, I think, than anything connected with public affairs in all my long experience.  It is a theme which I hope you will dwell upon; a theme which I hope and trust you will do your best to spread abroad in all parts of the world, so that from this date onwards for all time, we who speak the common language and have these common ideals may feel that we are working not merely for ourselves individually, nor even for our joint interests, but that we are working together for the best interests of the whole of mankind and for the civilisation of not only the Old World but of the New.

## ADDRESS TO THE ELECTORS OF THE CITY OF LONDON

### December 2nd, 1918

LADIES AND GENTLEMEN,—After twelve years of political service as member for the City, and nearly forty-five years of labour in the House of Commons, I beg to seek re-election at your hands. In all recorded time there has never been a pause of more compelling solemnity than the one in which I write. Behind us lies the Great War; before us looms the task of arranging peace, redrawing the boundaries of powerful States, freeing oppressed nationalities, rebuilding the shaken fabric of our industrial civilisation, and securing, if we can, the future of the world against the calamities from which we ourselves have so deeply suffered. As we look backward with gratitude, so we must look forward with hope. The horror of the last four years is over. We no longer dread the brutal menace of German domination; the treasure lavished without stint, the far more precious lives surrendered gladly in the cause of freedom, have not been spent in vain; for peace seems assured and the world again breathes freely. But we cannot content ourselves with counting up the sufferings and the glories of the past. The subject indeed is absorbing. The steadfast heroism of our seamen and soldiers, the admirable manner in which all classes in the community—I had almost said all the members of every class—have done their best to aid the common cause, will for long years supply unexhausted themes to the proud historians of our race. But we have other duties to fulfil. We must not merely dwell on the past, we must provide for the future; and it is of the tasks of the future that I would now speak, since it is only by your support and assistance that I can hope to take any share in their accomplishment.

The essential question the constituencies will have to answer in the next few weeks is this—To whom should be entrusted the task of co-operating with our Allies in framing a lasting international settlement, and to whom should be entrusted the heavy labours of national reconstruction? In other words, what Government and what parties would they wish to guide the country through the difficult transition from war to peace? If I appeal to them to give their votes in favour of the present Government and its supporters, this is not because I underrate the patriotism and capacity of other statesmen and other parties. Nor is it because I wish to claim for the Administration to which I belong any super-human immunity from errors and miscalculations. Yet, surely, if we take a broad view, we may look with legitimate pride on its performance. In circumstances of extraordinary difficulty it has developed, sometimes beyond all recognition, the work which its predecessors had begun; it has met new

dangers by new expedients; it has organised, or
borne its full share in organising, victory on every
front where Imperial Forces have been fighting,
whether in Asia, Africa, or Europe; it has dealt
successfully with the ever-growing strain of financing our own efforts in the war, and no small portion
of the efforts of our Allies.  Britain under its guidance has become a single, huge, co-ordinated
mechanism for producing armies and armaments,
ships and food, for guarding the waterways of the
world, for supplying to our friends, and denying
to our enemies, the materials required in modern
war.

Now the successful transition from war to peace
is as hard of execution, and as momentous in its
consequences, as the transition from peace to war;
and it requires similar qualities in those who are
called on to effect it.  Moreover, we must bear in
mind that the task in front of Britain and the
British Empire is in some respects more difficult
than that which any other country has to face.  If
the chief industry of a country is agriculture, if
most of its soldiers are peasants, peace means mainly
the return to their farms of those who formerly
cultivated them.  Outside the actual theatre of
military operations these farms are not derelict.
They may have suffered somewhat from lack of
labour and of fertiliser.  The ungrudging toil of
women and children, wonderful though it has been,
may not have made up for the absence of father and
brothers at the front. Yet during the War those
farms produced the same kind of things that they

produced before the War began; or that they will be called on to produce now that the War is over. There has been no breach of industrial continuity; no displacement of the industrial population. The case of Great Britain is very different. She is in the main a manufacturing country, peculiarly dependent on the import of raw materials, and the export of finished goods. The War has driven the whole of this productive energy into unaccustomed channels. Our existing plant has been used for new purposes; new plant has been erected on an enormous scale. When the armistice was declared our machines were making little except munitions, our labour was almost wholly devoted to war work, our ships were carrying nothing except under the direction of high military policy. To a degree unknown either in France or America, Italy or Japan, the energies of our pepole, when not actually engaged in fighting, were thus forcibly diverted from the arts of peace to those of war; and if now they have to be turned again into their former courses, the change cannot be made without difficulty, nor, I fear, without some suffering. If we would truly measure the magnitude of the difficulty we must, in the first place, bear in mind that four years of war have left us poorer by thousands of millions of accumulated wealth, and by so much the less able to accomplish reforms whose cost is great. In the second place, we must note that we are not concerned merely to bring back pre-war conditions. While we restore we must endeavour also to improve. In the third place, we must realise that although

the moral and political conditions under which
this endeavour has to be realised are full of
hope and encouragement, not all the symptoms are
clearly favourable. For the war provoked by German
ambitions has had consequences as tremendous as its
criminal contrivers anticipated, but very different
in their character. Defeat has shattered the military
prestige of Central and Eastern Europe; but militar-
ism in its fall has shaken to its foundation the social
fabric with which it was interwoven. Russia is in
a condition of septic dissolution. Many observers
tell us that the infection is spreading to Russia's immediate neighbours—to Hungary, to Austria, even
to Germany. Imperial Germany itself has gone into
voluntary liquidation, though whether the transaction be an honest one few would venture to assert.
However this may be, there is no political truth
more certain than that every great catastrophe is
apt to find an echo, however faint, in regions far
removed from the original centre of disturbance, and
there are those who fear that we shall not wholly
escape.

So far as I am concerned, however, I pronounce
myself an optimist. I have heard many prophecies
of evil in the course of my political life, and some
have come true. But the ones which have always
proved false are those which assumed that on great
occasions the British nation would prove unequal to
the task of working its institutions at home, or performing its duty overseas, with reasonable success.
Some able observers in the last century doubted
whether the honour of the country could be as safe

under modern political conditions as it has been in the brave days of old. The story of the last four years would have given them abundant consolation. An eminent friend and colleague of mine believed to his dying day that in questions of peace and war the women of England could not be trusted unswervingly to follow the hard path of patriotic sacrifice. Had he lived till 1918 assuredly he would have changed his mind. And as it has been in the past, so I believe it will be in the future. Our pride in the past is no ignoble prejudice; our hopes for the future are not fantastic dreams. Mr. Lloyd George and Mr. Bonar Law have stated on behalf of the Coalition the outlines of a constructive policy at once moderate and bold. I do not doubt that when Parliament meets and the time comes for filling in the outlines by administrative and legislative action, they will have behind them a House of Commons worthy to represent the will of the country at the great moment. It is my earnest desire that, by your favour, I also may be found among their supporters.

# 3

## On International Indebtedness

*Speech in the House of Lords, "to call attention to misunderstanding that has arisen respecting the Note\* on International Indebtedness of the First of August, 1922," March 8th, 1923*

My Lords, it may be in your Lordships' recollection that when I was in an official position I wrote, on behalf of the then Government, a Paper dealing with the most difficult, most dangerous, and most anxious question of the international indebtedness. It created some controversy at the time—a controversy in which I took no part—and I certainly thought that as time went on, and as with regard to this very question changes of momentous importance have taken place since August 1st of last year, the matter might have been allowed to rest. But I think you will agree with me that when so important a personage, a statesman so highly placed in an official position of such special importance in this connection as that of Ambassador to the United States, declared that a statement made by me in that Despatch is misleading, and that he publicly desires the present British Government formally and ex-

---

\*The text of this Note, known as "The Balfour Note," follows below.

plicitly to remove a misapprehension which that statement is said to have occasioned, silence on my part would probably lead to misunderstanding.

Now the sentences complained of occur in the following passage of the original Note:

"For it should not be forgotten, though it sometimes is, that our liabilities were incurred for others not for ourselves——"

that refers of course to our Debt to America, and to that alone—

"The food, the raw material, the munitions required by the immense naval and military efforts of Great Britain, and half the two thousand million sterling advanced to Allies were provided, not by means of foreign loans, but by internal borrowing and war taxation . . . . Appeal was therefore made to the Government of the United States; and under the arrangement then arrived at, the United States insisted, in substance if not in form, that, though our Allies were to spend the money, it was only on our security that they were prepared to lend it. This co-operative effort was of infinite value to the common cause; but it cannot be said that the rôle assigned in it to this country was one of special privilege or advantage."

That is the whole of the passage in which the extract complained of occurred.

The actual sentence which the Ambassador complained of runs as follows:

"Under the arrangement then arrived at the United States insisted, in substance if not in form, that, though our Allies were to spend the money, it was only on our security that they were prepared to lend it."

Now, my Lords, I am unable to find in these words anything which is either misleading or obscure. It is perfectly true that they are very compressed, and that without knowing all the circumstances of the case their full import may not be very easy to determine, but I do not think they deserve the strictures passed upon them by his Excellency.

The essential facts of the case are as follows: Up to America's entry into the War the burden of financing those Allies who could not adequately finance themselves fell mainly, though not wholly, upon Great Britain; and the most anxious and difficult part of our financial task in those early days of the War was that of finding dollars wherewith to pay the American producer for war materials required by ourselves and our friends. Of course, this state of things was changed by America's entry into the War, but her belligerency, which changed so much, naturally could not diminish the demand made for American war material in Europe, although through the operation of loans it most undoubtedly did diminish materially the difficulty of pay for this war material. Now the way the system worked was that, in essence, the American Government borrowed in America; that out of these internal loans the American producer was paid; and that one or other of the European belligerents (not necessarily the belligerent who was to use the material) became liable to the United States Treasury for the amount of the loan.

How did this system, which I thus roughly indicate, work out as between the different nations concerned?   In some cases the loan was a direct transaction between the United States and some particular Ally, such as France or Italy, and this is the origin of that international indebtedness between those countries and America to which, in the course of his speech, the American Ambassador particularly referred.   But the case of Great Britain was not so simple.   It was complicated by the fact that, unlike other European belligerents, we were straining our credit to finance our friends, and that, unlike America, we were making very large purchases on our own account of goods which we had to import from overseas; in other words goods which we imported from America.

Our case, you will observe, was thus differentiated, broadly speaking, both from the case of the other European belligerents and from the case of America itself.   We had, as it were, two tasks thrown upon us.   Either of these tasks we could have accomplished without assistance and without external borrowing; but we were not in a position to accomplish both at the same time—a fact which surely need surprise nobody who remembers the enormous loans which we had already made to other nations before America came in the War, and which we continued to make afterwards.

In these circumstances the British Government suggested to the Government of the United States that the latter should relieve us of the first of these two tasks, in other words, that as we had borne the main burden financing the European Allies in the earlier years of the War, America, who came fresh into the great struggle, might relieve us of that part of our difficulties; and we assured her that, in these circumstances, we should be able to find all the dollars necessary for purchasing our war material, without borrowing from her or from anybody else; we could find them out of our own resources, out of our own taxes, out of our internal loans.

Had the United States Government seen its way to adopt this plan there would, of course, have been no loan from America to Britain, many controversies would have been avoided, and international arrangements would have followed another course. But, for reasons which I am the last person to question, and which, I doubt not, were amply sufficient, the American Government declined to adopt our proposal, and the double burden, the character of which I have endeavoured to describe to your Lordships, was still borne by this country. The result has been that Great Britain had to borrow from the United States, using the American money thus obtained to pay the American producer, and employing her own resources, thus set free, to aid her Allies. In other words, the American producer obtained his price, the American lenders got British security, our Allies were helped through their financial difficulties, and we obtained their promise to pay.

As it seems to me, these transactions were not inaccurately, though, I admit, most imperfectly, summarised in the phrase to which objection has been taken.

I cannot help feeling, however, that, after all, there may be a deeper difference between the American Ambassador and myself on this subject than any mere criticism or rejoinder with regard to one particular phrase in the original document would lead one to expect. The American Ambassador, as I understand it, regards the financial arrangements between the partners in the Great War as so many isolated undertakings, to be separately considered and carried through one by one, as occasion offers. Not only is this policy (in his view) necessary if the sanctity of contracts is to be maintained, but he thinks that it confers actual benefits on the debtor himself by improving his general credit. Speaking with hesitation before so great an authority, I am inclined to a somewhat less commercial view.

The extraordinary circumstances of the War, the magnitude of the co-operative effort made by the Allied and Associated peoples, each contributing its utmost to an enterprise in which all alike were interested, might seem to remove their financial arrangements into a sphere where the ordinary categories of debtor and creditor, though still valid, can hardly be deemed to be sufficient. Both views have something to recommend them; both may be held by honourable men. I do not propose to compare them, still less to criticise those who differ from me. But one final observation I may permit myself. If, as

I suppose, it is the first of these competing views which commends itself to public opinion in the United States of America, the uncontested and incontestable legal rights of that country could not have been enforced in a manner less likely to injure the happy relations which, I am glad to say, prevails between the two peoples.

# 4

## THE "BALFOUR NOTE," *August 1st, 1922*

Foreign Office,
August 1st, 1922.

YOUR EXCELLENCY—As your Excellency is aware, the general question of the French debt to this country has not as yet been the subject of any formal communication between the two Governments, nor are His Majesty's Government anxious to raise it at the present moment. Recent events, however, leave them little choice in the matter, and they feel compelled to lay before the French Government their views on certain aspects of the situation created by the present condition of international indebtedness.

Speaking in general terms, the war debts, exclusive of interest, due to Great Britain at the present moment amount in the aggregate to about £3,400,-000,000, of which Germany owes £1,450,000,000, Russia £650,000,000 and our Allies £1,300,000,000. On the other hand, Great Britain owes the United States about a quarter of this sum—say, £850,000,-000 at par of exchange, together with interest accrued since 1919.

No international discussion has yet taken place on the unexampled situation partially disclosed by these figures; and, pending a settlement which would go to the root of the problem, His Majesty's Government have silently abstained from making any demands upon their Allies, either for the payment of interest or the repayment of the capital. But, if action in the matter has hitherto been deemed inopportune, this is not because His Majesty's Government either underrated the evils of the present state of affairs or because they are reluctant to make large sacrifices to bring it to an end. On the contrary, they are prepared, if such a policy formed part of a satisfactory international settlement, to remit all the debts due to Great Britain by our Allies in respect of loans, or by Germany in respect of reparations. Recent events, however, make such a policy difficult of accomplishment.

With the most perfect courtesy, and in the exercise of their undoubted rights, the American Government have required this country to pay the interest accrued since 1919 on the Anglo-American debt, to convert it from an unfunded to a funded debt, and to repay it by sinking fund in twenty-five years. Such a procedure is clearly in accordance with the original contract. His Majesty's Government make no complaint of it. They recognise their obligations, and are prepared to fulfil them. But, evidently, they cannot do so without profoundly modifying the course which, in different circumstances, they would have wished to pursue. They cannot treat the repayment of the Anglo-American loans as if it were an isolated incident in which only the United States of America and Great Britain had any concern. It is but one of a connected series of transactions in which this country appears sometimes a debtor, sometimes as creditor; and if our undoubted obligations as a debtor are to be enforced, our not less undoubted rights as a creditor cannot be left wholly in abeyance.

His Majesty's Government do not conceal the fact that they adopt this change of policy with the greatest reluctance. It is true that Great Britain is owed more than it owes, and that if all inter-Allied war debts were paid the British Treasury would on balance be a large gainer by the transaction. But can the present world situation be looked at only from this narrow financial standpoint? It is true that many of the Allied and Associated Powers are as between each other creditors or debtors or both, but they were and are much more. They were partners in the greatest international effort ever made in the cause of freedom, and they are still partners in dealing with some at least of its results. Their debts were incurred, their loans were made, not for the separate advantage of particular States, but for a great purpose common to them all, and that purpose has been in the main accomplished. To generous minds it can never be agreeable, although for reasons of State it may perhaps be necessary, to regard the monetary aspect of this great event as a thing apart, to be torn from its historical setting and treated as no more than an ordinary commercial dealing between traders who borrow and capitalists who lend. There are, moreover, reasons of a different order to which I have already referred which increase the distaste with which His Majesty's Government adopt so fundamental an alteration in method of dealing with loans to Allies.

The economic ills from which the world is suffering are due to many causes, moral and material, which are quite outside the scope of this dispatch. But among them must certainly be reckoned the weight of international indebtedness, with all its unhappy effects upon credit and exchange, upon national production and international trade. The peoples of all countries long for a speedy return to the normal. But how can the normal be reached while conditions so abnormal are permitted to prevail? And how can these conditions be cured by any remedies that seem at present likely to be applied? For, evidently, the policy hitherto pursued by this country of refusing to make demands upon its debtors is only tolerable so long as it is generally accepted. It cannot be right that one partner in the common enterprise should recover all that she has lent, and that another, while recovering nothing, should be required to pay all that she has borrowed. Such a procedure is contrary to every principle of natural justice, and cannot be expected to commend itself to the people of this country.

They are suffering from an unparalleled burden of taxation, from an immense diminution in national wealth, from serious want of employment, and from the severe curtailment of useful expenditure. These evils are courageously borne, but were they to be increased by an arrangement which, however legitimate, is obviously one-sided, the British taxpayer would inevitably ask why he should be singled out to bear a burden which others are bound to share.

To such a question there can be but one answer, and I am convinced that Allied opinion will admit its justice. But while His Majesty's Government are thus regretfully constrained to request the French Government to make arrangements for dealing, to the best of their ability, with Anglo-French loans, they desire to explain that the amount of interest and repayment for which they ask depends, not so much on what France and other Allies owe to Great Britain, as on what Great Britain has to pay America.

The policy favoured by His Majesty's Government is, as I have already observed, that of surrendering their share of German reparation and writing off, through one great transaction, the whole body of Inter-Allied indebtedness. But if this be found impossible of accomplishment, we wish it to be understood that we do not in any event desire to make a profit out of any less satisfactory arrangement. In no circumstances do we propose to ask more from our debtors than is necessary to pay to our creditors. And while we do not ask for more, all will admit that we can hardly be content with less; for it should not be forgotten, though it sometimes is, that our liabilities were incurred for others, not for ourselves.

The food, the raw material, the munitions required by the immense naval and military efforts of Great Britain, and half the £2,000,000,000 advanced to Allies were provided not by means of foreign loans, but by internal borrowing and war taxation.   Unfortunately a similar policy was beyond the power of other European nations; appeal was therefore made to the Government of the United States, and under the arrangement then arrived at the United States insisted, in substance if not in form, that though our Allies were to spend the money, it was only on our security that they were prepared to lend it.   This co-operative effort was of infinite value to the common cause, but it cannot be said that the rôle assigned in it to this country was one of special privilege or advantage.

Before concluding, I may be permitted to offer one further observation in order to make still clearer the spirit in which His Majesty's Government desire to deal with the thorny problem of international indebtedness.

In an early passage of this dispatch I pointed out that this, after all, is not a question merely between Allies; ex-enemy countries also are involved, for the greatest of all international debtors is Germany. Now, His Majesty's Government do not suggest that either as a matter of justice or expediency Germany should be relieved of her obligation to the other Allied States.   They speak only for Great Britain, and they content themselves with saying once again that so deeply are they convinced of the economic injury inflicted on the world by the existing state of things that this country would be prepared (subject to the just claims of other parts of the Empire) to abandon all further rights to German reparation and all claims to repayment by Allies provided that this renunciation formed part of a general plan by which this great problem could be dealt with as a whole, and find a satisfactory solution. A general settlement would, in their view, be of more value to mankind than any gains that could accrue even from the most successful enforcement of legal obligations.

I have, etc.,

BALFOUR.

# 5

## ON THE LEAGUE OF NATIONS

*Speech in the House of Commons, June 18th, 1920*

THE League of Nations suffers, perhaps, from criticism of various kinds more than is quite just or reasonable. We have two sets of enemies besides our candid friends. Of our candid friends I say nothing. Candid friends are in every walk of life. Mankind has suffered from them from the beginning of time, or at all events from the time of Job downwards, and no one has yet found a very satisfactory method of dealing with them. I do not mean to add my mite or my contribution to the failure of centuries.

The first set of enemies are those who frankly dislike the League. Sometimes they are what are called men of the world. A man of the world usually is a man who believes nothing good of the world, and who not only believes nothing good of the world, but does not think that the world is capable of improvement. I share neither of those views. It is perfectly true in one sense that you will not within measurable centuries alter the raw material of human nature. It is there, and you have to make the best of it. But do not tell me that, because the raw material of human nature remains unchanged, human society is never to be improved. It is not only contrary to all faith and hope, but contrary to all experience.

I believe that if the League, that is the nations working in concert through the League, really have the insight and the patriotism to use the machinery which they have created to the best of their ability, you will gradually build up a state of public feeling which, in the absence of any positive sanction, will make such disasters as we have gone through in the last five years absolutely impossible. That is the answer I would give to my friend the man of the world, who, I am sure, would be most uncomfortable if you made him travel from London to York in the same conditions of security now, as those in which his great-grandfather travelled at the end of the eighteenth century or the beginning of the nineteenth century. It is quite obvious that you can improve the structure of society.

Then among the enemies, I have to count those who, in some mysterious way, have persuaded themselves that war is a great moraliser. Of course all misfortunes can be turned to good account. Disease, in that sense, is a great moraliser; poverty in that sense may be a great moraliser. There are natures who, in a time of trial, rise to heights which perhaps they did not themselves dream of before the trial came. But if any sane man thinks that that is the road to progress, if he thinks that by multiplying misfortunes you are going to promote morality, he surely should meditate upon his theories within the boundaries of an asylum rather than attempt to add them to the general stock of national wisdom.

There is the last class of open enemy, who have
a sort of semi-moral, semi-scientific varnish with
which they cover their strange creed.  Having read
in their Darwin that there is a struggle for existence,
and that through that struggle for existence a great
many important morphological developments have
occurred, they seem to think that a state of universal
warfare is really the best method of attaining universal progress.  They entirely mistake Darwin, and
they entirely mistake morality, and they talk a sort
of nonsense which, I regret to say, a great many
people who should have known better talked in Germany.  But they had a reason for talking it; they
wanted to justify universal domination, and by the
struggle for existence, in which the best survived,
they meant the struggle between Germany and the
world, in which Germany survived.  But the gentlemen of whom I speak have no such reason, and they
do nothing but harm by spreading this sham philosophy among the young and ignorant.

Much more dangerous, in my opinion, even than
these enemies, are the people who do not object to
the League because it goes too far, but who object
to the League because, in their opinion, it does not
go far enough.  They think it is so powerless as to
be utterly contemptible.  If they are allowed to have
their way, they will destroy the League altogether.
Their view is that there should be great naval,
military, and air forces at the bidding of the League,
to be used, I suppose, at a moment's notice as soon
as any threat of war occurred, and they want those
to be levied by compulsory action on the members of

the League, so that they want to create a super-State armed with all the military trappings of a military empire. The League of Nations would cease to be a league of nations, and would become a series of subordinate States under one super-State. Those who framed the Covenant had no such notion in their minds. Their whole view was of a different character, and I am quite confident they were right. This problem did not go unconsidered at the Paris Conference. I was not a member of the Committee which dealt with these things, but I know they most carefully considered it and absolutely rejected it.

Please remember, if the League of Nations is not a world-league more than one-half of its value goes. One great nation is at present standing out of the League. I neither criticise nor inquire into the motives which make that policy, but undoubtedly one of the motives that induced America to pause before she entered the League was the idea that her national sovereignty was fatally or dangerously interfered with. Yet with the tremendous instance before them of the evil done by over-pressing the claims of the League there are enthusiasts for it who say that it is no use unless you create over the sovereign States of the world some super-State which is to direct the forces levied, paid for, officered by those sovereign States, and is to control the free governments of free peoples, subject only, I suppose, to an occasional meeting of the League in full conference and such check as the Council of the League may conceivably impose. I think those schemes are really wild, and nobody who tries to carry them out can

come to any other conclusion.  It is not easy to work
a few nations together in one theatre of war; but
if you are going to work five and forty nations,
speaking forty languages, how are you going to
house them, recruit for them, pay for them, officer
them, direct them, staff them?  The thing really
breaks down at once.  You cannot rule the world
in this way.  It is not the plan of the League of
Nations, and, believe me, it is not a plan with which
the League of Nations is compatible for a year.

What are the weapons which the League is asked
to use?  What are the means which you put at its
disposal?  They are not fleets, armies, and air forces.
The two main instruments are delay and publicity.
These are not instruments which you can use in the
middle of a great crisis; they are instruments to use
in a peaceful world which somebody desires to disturb.  Delay, discussion, publicity, public opinion,
commercial boycott and arbitration, and if they fail,
and in the last resort, then military measures—that
is an admirable system, but not for dealing with all
the eventualities which are before our eyes or all
the troubles from which we are suffering.  Quite the
contrary.  No rational man would suggest that the
League is constituted to deal with the world, or any
part of the world, which is in chaos.  That must be
dealt with either by the Supreme Council or in other
ways.

The League may give assistance, but the League
is not, and cannot be, a complete instrument for
bringing order out of chaos. Those who would
throw upon it that burden in the name of peace and

of co-operation among civilised peoples are doing
the greatest disservice to the League of Nations.
The League of Nations will serve you well if you
do not overload it.  At least that is my hope, my
faith.  If you overload it you will assuredly break
it down.  Even now it is maimed and crippled by the
fact that unhappily we have not so far succeeded in
inducing the United States to take part in our
labours.  If you either allow the League of Nations
to be used as an instrument by the free nations of
the world in their own party warfare, or if they try
to throw upon it burdens which it is ill-fitted to bear,
on them will be the responsibility of destroying the
most promising effort in the direction of the renewal
of civilisation which mankind has ever yet made.

# 6

## ON THE LEAGUE OF NATIONS

*Statement Broadcasted by Lord Balfour on Friday,*
*October 10th, 1924*

I HAVE been asked to speak briefly on the changes
which the League of Nations has made, or may
make, in the methods of dealing with international
relations. The time at my disposal is short. But
I have a yet more fundamental difficulty to contend
with. The League has only had an effective existence of about five years, a mere moment in the
history of the world. This is far too brief a period
for adequately testing the merits of what was ad-
mittedly a great experiment. It is true that theorists
in abundance had toyed with the idea which the
League embodies; but practical statesmen fight shy
of Utopias, and it required the terrors and troubles
of the Great War to induce the nations to make
trial of a scheme at once so ambitious and so new.
Our views on it, therefore, must be provisional, as
our relevant experience has been brief; but let me
add with all emphasis that, though provisional, they
ought in my opinion to be most favourable.

In endeavouring to form a judgment as to the
future of the League and its effect on the conduct
of international affairs, we must remember that it

is in danger from two quarters. It is in danger from its embittered enemies; it is perhaps in still greater danger from its indiscreet friends. The first think it will produce a weakening of national sentiment, a decay of patriotism, and an increasing reluctance to make the personal sacrifices and undergo the personal perils which the defence of Empire may involve. Defence (say these critics) will henceforth be thought unnecessary, and in any case will be the business, not of particular nations, but of the League as a whole. Such a consummation is depressing enough, but its gloom is deepened in the eyes of those pessimists by the fact that, in their opinion, it is based on a dangerous delusion. The League, they think, will never be able to carry out its mission. It will never succeed in maintaining the peace of the world. From these premises they draw the melancholy conclusion that the pacific nations who believe in League principles will place a quite excessive reliance upon its power to protect them, and will consequently become morally and materially far less able to protect themselves; whilst the aggressive nations—whether members of the League or not—who are wholly alien to its spirit, and are still filled with the lust of domination, will find in it an unsuspecting ally who has skilfully prepared the way for their cherished schemes of aggression.

These fears seem to me to be quite illusory. It is true, no doubt, that the whole atmosphere of the League tends to make the separate nations of which it consists more conscious that, in spite of all their differences, they have common interests, common duties, and share a common life. But I see not the least reason for supposing that this will weaken the true patriotism, or diminish in the smallest degree the vigour of national life. Nor yet will it imperil national defence unless we fall into the error of supposing that because we believe ourselves to have brought a machinery into existence which, if properly used, will provide a powerful safeguard against the horrors of war, we may thereafter sit still and congratulate ourselves on having successfully started the millennium. The machine may be a good one, but no machine works by itself; and the future of the League must depend not merely upon the excellence of its constitution, but upon the spirit in which its provisions are turned to account. It is the boast of the League that it exists to do something which, though often desired, has never yet been attempted. But the very height of this ideal is a measure of its difficulty. It is folly to suppose that the task prescribed at Versailles is an easy one; still greater folly to expect that in carrying it out no mistakes will be made. In the long run mistakes are inevitable; and when they occur we may perhaps discover that the loudest acclaimers of the Great Experiment are not among its most constant friends.

But you will perhaps press me to explain in more detail wherein the present machinery for conducting international affairs differs from, and improves upon, that which prevailed before the War. Let me say, in the first place, that the new differs from the old not by substitution, but by addition. No existing method of dealing with foreign relations has been either destroyed or weakened. Diplomacy in the hands of Secretaries of State and the Ambassadors and Ministers who carry out their instructions has lost neither in prestige nor in value. Conferences, like that which met at Washington in 1921-22, remain what they have always been—an invaluable, though doubtless far from perfect, method of dealing with special questions under special circumstances. The principle of arbitration has gained, not lost, by what has occurred at Geneva. The authority and the effectiveness of international law has been strengthened, not weakened, by the establishment, under the auspices of the League, of the Court of International Justice at The Hague. Now all these things, except the last, belong to "the old diplomacy," and even the last might perhaps be claimed as a development of its methods. Whilst, therefore, we must all admit that in the hands of unscrupulous politicians it has sometimes been turned to unscrupulous account, the fact remains that we cannot do without it; and most certainly the world is, and always has been, the better for its existence.

Assured as I am of this truth, I am not less confident that no mere modification of these time-honoured methods can provide a substitute for the machinery of the League. For this possesses three characteristics which are entirely novel.

It has a permanent (and, I may add, a very able) staff, which, though itself without executive authority, makes it practicable for the League to undertake duties which involve continuing responsibilities; for example, those connected with Danzig and the administration of the mandated territories.

It has a powerful and independent organ in the shape of its Council, which meets often, and if need arose could meet still oftener, for the purpose of carrying on its current business, and dealing at short notice with any international crisis with which the League might be confronted.

And finally it has its Assembly where the representatives of more than fifty nations meet together in free and friendly co-operation.

All these different portions of the machine are essential to its working; all of them are of the first importance; all of them are new, and collectively they constitute an organ of international opinion whose possible value is hard to over-estimate. And please note that this judgment is not based on speculative prophecy. It rests on facts already experienced. During the five years of the League's existence the variety and importance of its undertakings have been most remarkable. I attempt no list of them; but, in addition, to settling international differences, they include financial reconstructions (as of Austria and Hungary); the safeguarding of Western Europe from the invasion of disease; the control of certain international waterways; the protection of minorities in certain areas; the superintendence of mandated territories; and the suppression of vicious, and the control of dangerous, forms of international traffic. These enterprises were all of them difficult, and all of them important. The measure of success achieved has been great, and I doubt whether any of them would have been attempted had the League not been in existence.

Let me conclude with an endeavour to describe a great and, as I think, most valuable characteristic of the League which could not have been anticipated with certainty from a mere examination of its paper constitution. Every impartial spectator who has had the opportunity of watching the League in session must, I think, have been impressed, as I have been, by the moral atmosphere if its own creation in which it carries on its work. This is quite unlike anything to be found elsewhere—a fact in itself not very surprising, since elsewhere no similar body exists.

The representatives of over fifty separate communities, drawn from every quarter of the globe, containing members of all the great divisions of mankind, speaking every great language (except Russian), professing many religions, nurtured in widely different traditions, all citizens of States whose history books are filled with accounts of injuries mutually inflicted, are collected to the number, I suppose, of some one hundred and forty in a town about as large as Brighton. All of them are men of note in their own community, well accustomed to deal with public affairs. Not a few are of world-wide reputation. For some weeks of strenuous labour they and their staff constitute a society which is almost self-contained. In the Assembly and in Committees, in public and in private, during the long hours of business and the brief hours of leisure, they are in personal touch with each other, and rarely in touch with anyone else. Speaking broadly, they approach the questions submitted to them undivided by party, unhampered by narrow and selfish considerations. No doubt every member represents his own particular State, and never forgets the fact. But neither does he forget his membership of the body to which he is temporarily attached, whose labours he shares, whose policy he may influence, to whose collective quality he cannot but contribute. Such a body could not but create an atmosphere of its own; and the world would be singularly unfortunate or singularly ill-directed if that atmosphere is not found favourable to the friendly solution of the most perplexing international problems, and the peaceful settlement of the bitterest international disputes.

## 7

ON THE LOCARNO TREATIES AND THE LEAGUE OF
NATIONS

*Speech in the House of Lords, November 24th,
1925*

IF anybody wants to realise what the stage in the
gradual healing of Europe is, which is marked and
caused by the Locarno Treaty, let them cast their
minds back even a very few years, and ask themselves whether it was then conceivable that there
should meet round an equal table the representatives
of Germany, of Italy, of France, of Belgium and
ourselves in friendliest converse, dealing with perfect sympathy and comprehension, and ultimately
perfect agreement, with the difficult international
problems which the Locarno Treaty embodies.
Is it possible to conceive such an event taking place, if you put yourselves into the frame
of mind in which the different States of Europe
found themselves when other influences were at
work, other statesmen were at the head of affairs,
and when fear and hatred were almost the domi-
nant passions that influenced the policy of some great
nations?

When I say that the change has been great, I
do not suggest that there has been any great change

in the movement of public opinion in this country. So far as I am able to estimate the opinions of my fellow-countrymen and the actions of preceding Governments, they have always been anxious for appeasement. Each in its several ways, and to the best of their abilities, and according to the opportunities that circumstances offered them, has striven for the same end for which we have striven in the Locarno Treaty; and indeed the work of the Treaty of Locarno is based largely upon previous work done by those who were in office before the present Government came into power.

I speak not of British public opinion, but of Continental public opinion, and I speak with perfect confidence, when I say that it is impossible to conceive the great work which has now, I hope, been accomplished, being brought to a satisfactory conclusion, in the spiritual conditions which prevailed, relatively speaking, but a few months ago. That is an immense change. It is a change infinitely for the better, and I cannot help thinking that the public instinct is not deceived when it regards the Treaty of Locarno as the symbol and the cause of a great amelioration in the public feeling of Europe, as the beginning of a new era, as the end of an old and evil state of things, as the first great step towards that international amity which scarcely differs more from a state of overt war than it differs from the moral bitterness which prevailed, uninterfered with and unchecked, for so many years after peace was nominally concluded.

I am not going to describe the Treaty. But

there are two broad points on which, perhaps, I
may say a word.  The first relates to the League
of Nations.  It has been suggested that, disguise
it as you will, the Treaty of Locarno is really a
blow aimed, not intentionally but in effect, at the
League of Nations; that the Treaty of Locarno, as
it were, puts aside the League of Nations as the
guardian of peace and the arbiter of harmony, and
substitutes for it what may be relatively described
as a private arrangement between certain great
Powers from which the League, excepting in name,
is obviously and manifestly excluded.

I think that is a very profound and even dangerous mistake.  We have to consider, of course, that
the League of Nations, as it is at present constituted,
is not in every respect the League of Nations as
designed by its original framers.  It differs from
that original plan not merely because certain great
nations have declined to belong to it, although that
fact does make an important difference in certain
aspects of the League's potential activity.  I do not
think it has made any difference in the work which
the League has actually done, and nobody who has
studied what the League has done will, in my
opinion, be inclined to underrate the immense and
growing services which it is doing to international
relations and civilised society.  I believe that those
benefits are enormous, and I do not think they could
have been better performed even if all the nations
of the world had, as was originally hoped and
planned, made themselves members of the League.

It is not, therefore, what has been done, or what

is being done, which causes anxiety to those who, like myself, think that the future of the world, and of civilisation, very largely depends upon the prestige and the growing power of the League of Nations. Their anxiety is not due, as far as I am aware, to their thinking that the League has defeated the designs of its framers in the way it has carried out the functions entrusted to it.  It may have made mistakes.  I am not aware of any human institution, national or international, which does not make mistakes, but, broadly speaking, I boldly say that any man who will take the trouble—and very few critics of the League do take the trouble—to see what the League has done, and is doing, will take the view that it is an immense, novel and effective addition to the machinery of international civilisation.  But behind that conviction there has always lurked the fear that, seeing that several great nations are not members of the League, and are not bound in any way by pledges to the League or by Treaties, the time might come when one, or all of them, might show a complete indifference to League ideals, might show a profound contempt for the power of the League, and might in one reckless moment undo the fabric so laboriously and so successfully being built up at Geneva.

That danger, be it real or be it imaginary, can only be cured or dealt with by considering a situation which, I hope and believe, is temporary, by looking around and seeing where in the community of nations this danger is likely at all to arise, and then by dealing with that danger to the best of your ability. I will not say that that is all that has been done, but it is one of the things which have been done at Locarno. Undoubtedly it would be mere affectation to deny that the international relations in the west of Europe and the centre of Europe did give rise to these anxious forebodings, but I believe they have been completely put an end to, so far as the great belligerents are concerned, by the Treaty of Locarno. In other words, this Agreement has underpinned what is temporarily the weakest part of the League of Nations.

If you say to me: "Well, cannot you imagine an international system in which such arrangements as those embodied in the Treaty of Locarno would find no place, in which all the work of preserving the peace would be thrown upon the League of Nations, unassisted by subsidiary international arrangements?"—of course I answer in the affirmative. I can easily conceive it. If you look forward to a time when every great nation will be a willing and a fervent adherent of the League of Nations and engaged in practising its principles, I think it is quite likely that such arrangements as are embodied in the Treaty of Locarno will become entirely antiquated, wholly superfluous, and will in the future be looked upon as having been merely a necessary stage in the general peaceful evolution of mankind. And no one would rejoice more than the authors of the Treaty of Locarno at such a consummation.

# SECTION VII
# GOLF

I

## On Origins and the American Golfers

*Speech at The Pilgrims' Luncheon in honour of the
United States golfers, May 14th, 1923*

LORD DESBOROUGH has justly said that I jumped
at the offer to take a share in the entertainment.
The fact is, this is the only luncheon, at any rate
the only semi-public occasion of a luncheon involv-
ing speeches, at which I should ever think of jump-
ing.  More august occasions possibly may have
presented themselves for subjects which were
supposed to be of world-wide importance, but I do
not think any subject is of more world-wide importance than golf.  I do not think any exponents of
golf more distinguished than our guests of this afternoon have ever appeared on these shores.  I imagine
that the ground of the chairman's invitation to me
to be present is because, in the first place, I am the
oldest member of the company by a long way, and,
in the second place, because I have a memory of the
world birth of golf which probably hardly anyone
else in this room can rival.

It is really a most extraordinary story, that story
of golf.  Here is a game which has been eagerly
played, and persistently played, for centuries by my
Scottish countrymen just across the Border, at a

distance from London much less than that which separates Boston from New York.

It was legislated against by the Scottish Parliament on the ground that it prevented Scotsmen from learning archery to fight the English. It went on persistently and uninterruptedly, and yet it never took root in this country, real root, and it never traversed the ocean, until well within my recollection. I am in the very centre of the world movement of golf. When we reflect that the oldest club in the world was an English club founded by Scotsmen who came with James the First from Scotland—I believe before the *Mayflower* started for America—a club which is still in existence at Blackheath—and that it has gone on for these centuries, and that there were one or two other great centres of golf in England, the English ignorance and indifference to the game in the past were perfectly extraordinary. One high authority was supposed to have described it as "Scotch croquet."

Then suddenly in the early 'eighties a movement began which has covered England with golf courses, which has covered America with golf courses, and which has made golf a game which is played wherever the English language is spoken, and in many places where the English language is not spoken, but which people speaking it frequent.

That sudden change is to me still an absolutely unexplained mystery, but whether it is capable of explanation or not, the fact is there; it is a great fact, and the greatest element of the fact in its development is the share which our English-speaking brothers in America have taken in its immense growth. They have adopted it, have carried the game to the highest pitch of perfection, and they have now for generations sent over to this country, and I hope will continue to send over, exponents of the game who cannot be excelled in any department of it.

Surely this is, from every point of view, to all those who love games as I do, one of the greatest and most satisfactory features in a period in which, if I may trespass beyond the realm of games, is not wholly satisfactory in all its aspects. But that aspect is wholly satisfactory. Here we have this magnificent game spread all over the world; here we have representatives from America coming over to Great Britain in 1923, as representatives of Great Britain go over to America, fighting out their battles in the spirit of true sportsmen and raising thereby the whole standard of games to the level which they ought to occupy.

What do I mean by playing the game as true sportsmen? I mean that, however much interest and flavour may be added to the contest by the fact that it is between America and Great Britain, or between Scotland and England, or this county and that county, or this State and that State—the fundamental thing is the game. That is the attitude in which true sportsmen approach it; that is the attitude in which they win or lose as the accident of fate or fortune may determine, and for many reasons, perhaps first because I think we have here the most admirable representatives not only of the game itself but of the way it should be played, I ask you to drink with all enthusiasm the health of our most distinguished guests.

## 2

ON "DOES GOLF DO MORE GOOD THAN HARM?"

*Speech in reply to Mr. Leo Maxse in a Debate on
the question: "Does Golf do more good than
harm?" May 14th, 1925*

GOLF was brought into England long before I had
any influence in encouraging its popularity. When
King James I came to London, the courtiers who
accompanied him from Scotland started a golf club
at Blackheath.

This gave Englishmen a chance, and it is to the
eternal discredit of the perception of the inhabitants
of the southern part of the island that, having this
model of a game before their eyes, they remained
impervious to the merits of an innocent and helpful
pleasure capable of good to young and middle-aged
alike. We had to wait until the last two decades of
the nineteenth century before golf began to get a
grip on the public in this country, and to spread
from here to every part of the world where the
English tongue is spoken. This was a reproach; but
I may say, "Better late than never." If England
was long in picking up the riches which lay at her
feet for the taking, she has amply made up, and she
and her sons in every part of the world now know
of the game, and largely play the game, and people

in many cases would no more think of travelling without the necessary equipment of golf clubs, than they would think in these days of travelling without a passport.

What is the criticism Mr. Maxse directs against the game? Mr. Maxse resents it largely because it is a game which a middle-aged man can play and can enjoy. Why should we have this attack on middle-aged men? Why this depreciation of their interest and of the pleasure they pursue?

I speak impartially because I am no longer middle-aged myself, but I am young enough to remember what I was like when I was a middle-aged man, and I well remember that in certain great essentials there is no game which, so far as hard-worked men are concerned, will give them the healthful satisfaction which they will derive from golf. We are always talking of shortening the hours of labour—a very proper object. But there is another object as difficult to attain, and that is a way to occupy the leisure which shortening the hours of labour is intended to produce.

If anybody will cast their minds back and think of their own experience, and contemplate the fate of a poor middle-aged man taken to the seaside by his wife and family, with no better occupation than to see his children dig castles in the sand or bathe, with no means of filling the weary hours of leisure, and will compare that state of things with the prospect of the same individual transported to a healthy climate and beautiful scenery, and with a game which will exercise all his skill to play moderately,

and much more than any skill he can perhaps produce to play the game supremely, he will admit that,
at all events, so far as the middle-aged man is concerned, the blessings of golf have been immense.

With regard to the younger generation, here
comes in, as I understand it, the sting of the criticism passed on golf by Mr. Maxse. He says that
boys at public schools and universities, who ought
to be better employed, are occupied in strolling somewhat lazily about the nearest golf course, never
exercising their limbs in rapid action, nor practising
their eyes in rapid judgment. He deduces from that
that this country has lost that supreme pride of
place in the matter of games which once it possessed.

I quite agree that there have been facts connected with international sports which I look at
with the same kind of regret that Mr. Maxse does,
but I would make two observations on that. Our
supremacy in games was not a supremacy inherent
in the physique of the British race. I am not aware
that we are more admirably equipped by nature for
success in games than our neighbours elsewhere.
Our success was obviously due to the fact that we
were the authors of all the great games in the world,
except baseball. That perhaps is not true of court
tennis, but we developed lawn tennis from court
tennis. It is from these shores that the passion for
football is extending. Cricket is purely of British
origin, and golf also had its origin in the British
Islands.

It is inevitable, if we are such good missionaries
of games as is indicated by the fact that we are

imitated and copied by other countries, that there must necessarily be interference with the solitary supremacy which once we possessed.  Our success as missionaries no doubt has prevented us from retaining that solitary supremacy of which we once could boast, but I think we have conferred an immense benefit on the world by the operation, whether the game be golf or lawn tennis.

Other nations have done us the honour to copy our Constitution in many cases, and it is not too much to say, if we compare their Constitutional practice with their practice in games, they have shown themselves much more skilful copyists of the second branch of human effort than of the first. We may boast without undue pride that it was from us that they learned the pleasure of the game and the practice of the game.

Golf is not a game which largely diverts our public school boys from cricket or football, rackets, or fives or other games. It is not largely played by our public schools.  Therefore you cannot put down any ill-success we may have to the fact that golf has proved an obstacle to our national prestige in international contests.  But I do think that public schools should encourage lawn tennis more than they do.  Lawn tennis is even more an international game now than golf.  In America, for instance, which has produced some of the greatest lawn tennis players that have existed, the game is played in the schools. It is absolutely discouraged in our own schools and is thought to be a game not appropriate to public school life, and not fitted to encourage public school

virtues.  The result is inevitable. Lawn tennis, like
golf, can only be practised with supreme success
by those who begin in their early youth.   I most
certainly wish that the authorities of the public
schools would wipe away the reproach that in a
game which we first developed we have not maintained the pride of place that I think we ought to
have maintained.

The mere fact that international financiers can
play golf and improve their figures, even if they
obtain no other advantage, is not a sufficient reason
for criticising a game which requires all that nature
has given us of muscular adaptation, accuracy of
eye and of judgment, delicacy of touch and of tem-
per.  I think the mere fact that some classes to which
Mr. Maxse has a strong objection get a good deal
of pleasure out of the game, is not a sufficient reason
for condemning it.

# INDEX